BEING IS ENOUGH

Collective Self-Help for a Sustainable World

Doug Brown

Hamilton Books
A member of
The Rowman & Littlefield Publishing Group
Lanham · Boulder · New York · Toronto · Oxford

Copyright © 2005 by
Hamilton Books
4501 Forbes Boulevard
Suite 200
Lanham, Maryland 20706
Hamilton Books Acquisitions Department (301) 459-3366

PO Box 317
Oxford
OX2 9RU, UK

Library of Congress Control Number: 2005929414
ISBN 0-7618-3268-8 (paperback : alk. ppr.)

For my wife, Beth, and my son and daughter, Mathieu and Sierra:

By their admirable actions and lifestyle they demonstrate to me that there is
a vital difference between
the joy one can receive from taking on challenges,
the fun one can have in accomplishing a goal,
and the fulfillment one can obtain from actualizing imagination
versus
the obsessive,
the compulsive,
the unthinking acceptance
of the cultural imperative of
be all you can be.

Contents

Illustrations

Preface

Being Is Enough is a sequel to *Insatiable Is Not Sustainable* (Westport, CT: Praeger Press, 2002), a statement of environmental philosophy that is as simple a message as the title suggests: if it's insatiable and knows no limits—whatever it is—it's not going to work for the future of humankind. *Insatiable*'s focus is on the destructive path of the global market and its support system: the evolving and increasingly globalized culture of "have all you can have" and "be all you can be." Its thesis is less straightforward and far more contentious than the title implies, however. The first part of the argument is widely accepted today: the have all you can have economy is destroying us and much of the community of life. The second part of the argument is what I've found to be controversial and intuitively resisted: the desire to have all you can have is a *result* of our desire to be all we can be.

With *Being* the focus is you. That's why its subtitle is "Collective Self-Help." This is a simple but atypical self-help book, in other words. But it's also about a new kind of "win-win" situation in which by helping to free yourself from an immense burden of stress and anxiety, you also help save the world—self-help for a sustainable world. The personal solutions that will save you will also save the world. No one cited, supported, and praised in this book, or looked to as a role model or example of how we can change is asking any of us to be altruistic or to be better than we are. *Being*'s hope is that we can remove some cultural blinders, set ourselves freer than we were, and find fulfillment in participating in whatever way we can in social change—in helping to create a socially and environmentally just world.

If you suffer stress, anxiety, fear, insecurity, a feeling of being overwhelmed much of the time, and a feeling of living a chaotic and frantic life, *Being*'s message will help liberate you from something no one wants to talk about. It's this: the world would actually work better if we quit trying to be all we can be. We can actually give up the obsession with self-development and self-actualization. Being is enough; we don't have to be more. Having to be more, since that is what society always tells us to do, is an unnecessary piece of cultural baggage. We can let it go, and by doing so we can also save the world. By giving up "productivism"—the be all you can be obsession—we can create a world of social justice, environmental sustainability, one that is motivated by being responsible participants in an economy energized by an ethic of maintenance rather than insatiable improvement.

And the remarkable thing is that it's not a tall order. Much of your stress is due to our world's fixation on having to always improve ourselves, our organizations, and what we mistakenly think is *our* world. Daniel Quinn made this point in *Ishmael*. As long as humans continue to act as if the world belongs to us, that we are supposed to use it to compulsively, improve how we survive, even when it comes at the expense of the life process itself, then we are in trouble.

But there's a growing movement, actually a worldwide movement of movements, that's hip to this. If you think that the social, political, and economic reforms are over the top, you're wrong. As I was preparing the *Preface* I was reading Ray Anderson's book, *Mid-Course Correction: Toward a Sustainable
Enterprise, the Interface Model* (Atlanta, GA: Peregrinzilla Press, 1998). Anderson is the CEO for the Interface corporation, the world's largest floorcovering
firm, and his book is his personal testimony of how his cultural blinders came
off. He didn't drop out of the business, but made a personal and corporate commitment to sustainable business practices. He stayed in and has succeeded. He is
a living testimony of the power of conversion and the ability of businesses to get
their social and environmental act together. So when folks say it can't be done,
here's one of many examples of where it's happening right in front of us.

Anderson mentions his experience as a college student in an economics
class, recalling the uncritical acceptance in the discipline that human wants are
insatiable. He states that we are led to believe that

> no matter what we have, we want more. That's human nature. More precisely,
> that's human nature in our culture, the culture that Daniel Quinn calls the
> 'taker' culture. Compound that with an ever-growing population, with each
> person wanting and striving for more, and it becomes clear that we have to find
> new, sustainable ways to satisfy needs and wants, other than by taking and tak-
> ing from Earth's limited capacity to provide from its stored natural capital, and
> other than by dumping our poison into her limited sinks. We just have to begin
> where we are, not where we wish we were—sooner, not later, according to the
> scientists—to take those first steps in the long journey to sustainability, and be-
> gin to dismantle the destructive, voracious, consuming technologies of the first
> industrial revolution. We must begin to reinvent business, commerce, and
> probably this whole civilization (something Daniel Quinn is trying hard to
> think through), and find ways to create wealth (perhaps redefine wealth), meet
> needs, satisfy wants, and raise standards of living for all without taking them
> out of Earth's hide.

One of the first steps taken by Interface in its effort to be a totally green business
was to introduce a new ethic: "doing well by doing good." Its point is obvious
but one that, again, many ideologues of capitalism and profit-maximization dispute: doing the right thing by putting the social interest first can actually further
the company's financial condition.

Americans are truly a population wedded to the idea that the unbridled pursuit of self-interest is what furthers the common good. Yet here is Ray Anderson
(and others discussed in *Being*) who is discovering that the opposite works better. Jeremy Rifkin's *The European Dream* makes a similar case for how Europeans are discovering, through the formation of the European Union, that by
pursuit of the general interest one's self-interest is maximized. This is ironic in a
sense, since it was a Scottish moral philosopher, Adam Smith, who first advanced the idea that self-interest works for the social betterment, and it was in

Europe that this principle, embodied in capitalism, was first tested. Now we find that Europeans are ready to move on by realizing that such a notion has become dysfunctional, while Americans continue to wear the blinders of individualism, competition, and self-interest. It shouldn't surprise us if the United States is the last bastion of untrammeled capitalism.

I'm reminded of a comment once made by Paul Sweezy (1910–2004), America's most famous Marxist economist, when asked about the difference between capitalism and socialism. He replied: "The purpose of capitalism is to beat the system, while the purpose of socialism is to make it work." Such an admission doesn't make Ray Anderson a socialist. That's not the point. Socialism, which continues to be my goal, doesn't have to be labeled as such since its principle is what matters. It will only come about when people realize that they have more to gain by justly working together than they do by competing with each other. Ray Anderson understands that and so do many Europeans today. They are in good company. Martin Luther King Jr., Matahma Gandhi, and Albert Einstein, among millions of others since Marx, all came to this realization. And now around the world, millions more who have never read Marx, never heard the word, socialism, and know nothing about Einstein, Gandhi, and King are coming together through networks of grass-roots organizations, coops, nonprofits, and local movements. And the World Social Forum is only one such venue for galvanizing the new global movements.

It would be overenthusiastic to suggest that what they have in common is the rethinking of our cultural norm of be all you can be. Most question have all you can have and continue to hang on to be all you can be. But we can let that go, as well. Giving up the productivist imperative, at least understanding how it affects you, will reduce your stress while making you feel better as a participant in helping to change the world. We want to create a world where everyone can get off of the performance-consumerist treadmill and still live justly, simply, and harmoniously with each other and the community of life, where quality of relationships is more satisfying than buying stuff. Of course, you won't have less stress if you don't have realistic expectations. As Albert Camus once said, "To believe that you can change the condition of humankind is insanity, but to refuse to try is cowardice." An economy and world not driven by insatiable social- and self-development is the biggest stress reliever we will ever discover. By trying to be more involved, change a few minds, and doing what you can, we can still have fun, be responsible, and live with less stress. We aren't cowards; we're simply finding meaning and purpose in trying to do the right thing. That's taking a cue from Ray Anderson, too.

Once you realize that it is the system that's your problem, that it is our modernist (or postmodernist) culture that's at the heart of your stress and insecurity, then changing the world makes sense and can be rewarding. As some would say, the material precondition for real stress-free living is the creation of a world that's not motored by stress. That's a world not driven by be all you can be—

insatiable development and improvement. Yet another huge challenge is looming: the current political climate is rife with "neocon" activists of the Right, many influencing the Bush administration, whose fundamental goal, climaxed with the attack on Social Security, is to make people as insecure as possible. Their vision is evidenced in a White House memo (January 3, 2005) by Peter Wehner, White House Director of Strategic Initiatives, and printed in the *Wall Street Journal*. The vision is of a world driven by the stress of insecurity such that everyone is compelled to ruthlessly compete, driving down wage costs, government entitlement costs, and freeing up labor markets to the benefit of business. The upside of this compete-or-die vision is that if it comes to pass, by its obvious inducement of an unprecedented condition of stress, people may get clear about something: the system is the problem. To free myself, I need to change the world. It would be better if it didn't have to come to that.

Acknowledgments

The first thank you and appreciation for support of this book must go to my Business College dean here at Northern Arizona University. Dean Mason Gerety has been both generous and supportive of this project. Clearly, without his financial support and confidence in my work, none of these ideas would have made it to my publisher. Additionally, I want to express my thanks and appreciation for the sabbatical leave granted me for the spring semester of 2005. This reprieve from classroom responsibilities has allowed me to complete *Being*, and I am grateful for that opportunity. It comes as a special privilege from the College of Business, my economics area coordinator, Professor Ron Gunderson, and the university's administration including the provost, Dr. Liz Grobsmith and our president, Dr. John Haeger.

Second, I want to thank Theresa Stacy-Ryan, Publication Specialist for the NAU College of Business. Her talent and skills, not to mention her creativity, were vital for the preparation of the camera-ready copy of the manuscript. We have worked together before, yet this book makes me appreciate even more her capabilities and skills with production editing. It has been a joy to have a collaborative association that humbles me with each conversation.

I also want to thank my wife, Beth, my son, Mathieu, and daughter, Sierra, for their unrelenting expressions of love and affection, without which this book would not have been written. They understand my motivations; we share a common conviction to change the world; and they are remarkable in their ability to overlook and ignore my grouchiness or discouragement, as unpredictable as these emotions frequently are.

Part One

You Don't Have To Be More

To Be or To Be More

A friend asked me about the title to this book. When I mentioned, *Being Is Enough*, he looked perplexed and suggested that if being was enough then nothing would get done, humans wouldn't be doing anything, and we'd all go extinct. I tried to explain that we are talking about the difference between being and becoming—that is, being versus being more. Being suggests that we go about living and doing what we need to do to live decent lives as individuals, communities, nations, and peoples. Becoming, on the other hand, is about being more tomorrow than you are today. It is about actualizing your potential as a human to always grow and develop your skills and capacities in ever new and unique ways. The *Mutts* comic strips have captured it.

© Patrick McDonnell. Reprinted with special permission of King Features Syndicate

In the first strip, "Mooch" ponders his to-do list and finds that it says, "Be All That You Can Be." And of course, this is number one on the list, much like we are told should be the priority in our own lives today. If you think of the to-do list as our culture, and even as our economy, it basically tells us that our lives are about one fundamental value: actualize your unlimited potential each and every day. Learn new skills, get more educated, accomplish more, achieve more, be ambitious, be goal-oriented, and with each new day, try to be more. Our society and our modern industrial culture tell us that the essential purpose of a human is to insatiably develop ourselves and our world. It tells us that we human beings are special, because we have the inherent capacity to always be more tomorrow than we are today. No other species in the community of life organizes itself either individually or collectively in an effort to be more and continually improve its condition.

Other life forms, we are told, only exist to survive. They are motivated by the need to survive. But they are not motivated by the need to improve *how* they survive. And they survive by doing the same thing over and over, endlessly repeating tomorrow what they did yesterday. Their attempts to survive can mean growth of the species and evolutionary adaptation over time, but they don't set about each day with the idea that they should improve and realize what potential they might have. This is clear in the second *Mutts* comic. The bee considers its list. It says, "just bee." In other words, go about your life, getting done what you need to do and just be a bee—"buzz" around and do what's necessary. You don't have to be more; being is enough. A colony of ants knows how to survive and clearly desires it. But they don't try to improve how they build their ant hills; they don't continuously seek new ways to find food. They simply repeat what's been genetically engineered within them. They do this because repetition works for them. All life forms other than humans are like this. What's different about us is that we are not content to repeat the old ways, as we know that whatever we've done or been can be improved upon. We are not content to survive. We are motivated by the limitless need to improve *how* we survive. Our motive is not merely survival but improvement. When I say, "being is enough," am I suggesting that we go back to living like bees and ants? Of course not. That's not a stress reliever. But there's value to their way of being and what we can learn from it. Moreover, their way of being was once ours.

We modern folk organize our lives and societies (with some exceptions) on the principle of continuous development and improvement. None of this is anything you don't already know, and that's why it's in *Mutts*—because we can relate to the difference between being and becoming. Humans evolved the idea that repetition doesn't work as well as the endless pursuit of improvement. Of course, what we feel compelled to repeat is the relentless quest for more. Modernity is repeating a theme that creates a tremendous dynamic of continuous change. Some would argue that it works for us in the same way that repetition of yesterday's ways works for other life forms. This book is about the fact that our repetitious insatiable obsession with being more has become dysfunctional. And it's causing you *unnecessary* stress, anxiety, insecurity, and frenzy.

Two hundred years ago at the beginning of the Industrial Revolution, capitalism was just an infant, but modern science was emerging, and economic growth was happening. Enlightenment intellectuals and scholars argued that humans should take advantage of this. The ability to insatiably self-realize and develop was a wonderful opportunity, they argued. With only a billion people on the planet and plenty of resources, who would think to question it? There was plenty of room, resources, and planetary recuperative power for everyone to go about becoming more and being insatiable.

But today there are six times that many people, and we are running out of resources. Humans are clearly pushing the earth's limits and carrying capacity. The social and environmental congestion from six billion people trying to insatiably develop is making us crazy. Not only do we suffer from personal stress, but we also suffer a kind of social stress. Contending with the consequences of others' insatiable self- and social-development is a problem. For example, the Chinese are doing a pretty remarkable job of growing their way to American affluence (Hertsgaard 2002, 1998). But it's not sustainable. For their 1.3 billion citizens to live like the average North American would require the carrying capacity of about four more planets. That's part of what defines social stress. We have to address the consequences of others' freedom to self-actualize. This is compounded by the fact that Americans with only five percent of the world's population are consuming a quarter of the world's resources and are creating that much of its pollution. Mark Hertsgaard calls China and the United States the world's "environmental superpowers." Between the two of them, they can make or break planetary sustainability. Social stress is the result.

We Have a Choice

The problem is that the survival motive of other sentient beings, like birds, animals, and marine life, is linked to satiability. Because their lives are all about being rather than becoming, they are more satiable in character. Being is a satiable thing, while becoming is not. Unlike them, our human motive of improvement is insatiable, so our becoming characteristic is linked to insatiability. Yet, humans do have a choice between being and becoming. Other species generally do not. Your dog, the birds in your yard, the bugs on your windshield—they have no choice. They are engineered to just be—to survive. Yet humans act as though they have no choice either: we have to become more, as if we were engineered to be insatiable improvers. But we do have a choice, and it's this choice between being and becoming that is special. It is not so much our compulsion to ever improve that makes us special, but our ability to choose how we live. It's the choice itself, between being satiable or not, that is unique to us. Unlike animals and birds in the community of life that have no choice, we can decide that being is enough or we can choose to always be more. It is only now, in the 21st century as we are made aware of global sustainability, limits to growth, and scarcity of resources that we would ever think about such a choice.

Humans have a pretty short history in a world that's 4.6 billion years old. For the first 99.5 percent of our past, we were like the bee in *Mutts*. We lived as hunters and gatherers from about 2 million years ago until 10,000 years ago. Then many, but not all, of us settled down to become farmers and build civilizations. We changed our ways and figured out that we could become more, have more, develop more, and achieve more. By the 16th century people pretty much decided that life as a human was different than the bees—we made "being more" the defining feature of our species. We scrapped the notion that being is enough and said, "Be all you can be." That was a choice modern humanity made. And it is essential to know something about how this happened if you are to understand your stress. By "choice" I mean that humans evolved in such a way that we began to view ourselves as these unique "becoming" creatures, and in effect, a cultural norm resulted that represents an unconscious shift in our self-definition from survivalists to improvers.

Even though we don't remember it as a choice, and even though we are led to believe that it wasn't a choice but an inherited attribute of our species, it was a choice. We have succumbed to a cultural dictate as if, like the ants, we are destined to repeat forever what we've only been for the last half a percent of our existence: to be is to always be all you can be. More importantly, this endless repetition that to be is to always be more is insatiable.

We made, in other words, insatiability the defining feature of our lives! This has become very stressful. It makes living an overwhelming ordeal rather than a simple and relaxed experience of harmony with people and nature. Maybe we need more and better technology to make life easier. Well, how much technology is enough? The 19th century philosopher and economist, John Stuart Mill, stated during the Industrial Revolution that "it is questionable if all the mechanical inventions yet made have lightened the day's toil of any human beings" (Mill 1966, 328). Almost two hundred years ago, he was aware of the problem that humans seek technological innovations merely to produce ever more of them. What happened to leisure? Americans in fact work more today than they did thirty years ago (Schor 1992). It's the treadmill of production that we need to rethink. It is becoming the treadmill of improvement for improvement's sake.

Another explanation for our stress and the fact that there appears to be no solution to it is the conventional belief that people are "fatally flawed." Daniel Quinn exposed this myth in *Ishmael*. That humans are fatally flawed is clearly a cynical view, as it suggests that we are victims of a genetic feature often associated with greed. Thus, we hear, "People have always been greedy, and they always will be." Our greedy human nature makes us individualistic and competitive, so we suffer stress. Consequently, there's no relief. We'll examine this. Even though insatiability, like greed, is something that we might admit "happened to us" through our evolution, it's important to see it as a trait that is not fixed in our genetic makeup. So we made the choice to be insatiable? Not literally, of course: it happened so slowly that we weren't aware of it. But we did it to ourselves as part of our cultural evolution. And now we can undo it.

Our insatiable character is not genetic but culturally created. The cultural assimilation of be all you can be is so ingrained, so thorough, and so totally bred into us, that it has the appearance of being genetic. We have a feeling that be all you can be is eternal and universal to all humans. It is us, and we are it. That's wrong. It was a choice we've forgotten that we made. And people don't talk about it, because we've never thought of it as a choice. What we believe or accept as "natural" to our species we rarely question. If you were to watch a continuously running video that captured the entire history of humankind from a million-and-a-half years ago to today, you would be able to see exactly how this happened. What you'd witness is the initial period of over a million years in which humankind was actually satiable, had no driving concern for improvement, and lived like the bee in *Mutts*.

Then with the Agricultural Revolution 10,000 years ago, you'd see people settling down and beginning to grope their way to a belief that humans are always capable of "more." But this awareness would only be occurring in pockets of civilization. The remainder of humanity, what we call indigenous people, would be as satiable as ever. In fact, as recently as 500 years ago, up to a third of humanity was living the traditional way of satiability—being has been enough for indigenous peoples (Gowdy 1998). Finally, with the emergence of capitalism in Europe in the 16th century, you'd watch people there begin to talk about how everyone can and should be all they can be. By the end of the 20th century, you'd hear, "Sure, it's human nature to pursue more. Haven't we always been that way?"

Consequently, we who are caught up in the endless march of civilization have forgotten two things: 1) that humans lived very sustainably for 99.5 percent of our past without feeling that they had to be constantly more, and 2) that many humans have continued to do so today. But they are a vanishing species, not because they've been willingly converted to the insatiable life, but because their traditional way is continually being undermined by the expansionary logic of civilization. They are surrounded by insatiability. Now to say that their way of life isn't worth living, because they aren't bent on insatiable improvement like the rest of us, is simply false. They have found that life is worth living; that it is meaningful, purposeful, and gratifying because of two things: the quality of their human relationships and their connectedness to nature and the community of life. That is the essential message of our ancestors and the reason to protect our indigenous communities.

Here's my pitch: if you are stressed and feel overwhelmed with life much of the time, it's not always been that way, and it doesn't have to always be that way. Mooch, in the comic strip, is likely to encounter stress as he sets out to be all he can be. On the other hand the bee is not. Stress takes many forms and is expressed in numerous ways. In the excellent book, *Affluenza* (2001), the authors talk about "possession overload," and "time scarcity," for example. We know what these are from our daily routines. On the other hand, maybe you can be convinced of one simple thing: being is enough to make this world work for all of us. We don't have to always be more. It's not necessary for a sustainable and well-functioning world that it be driven by improvement and insatiable self- and social-actualization.

Our fixation with insatiable development of both our personal selves and our social institutions is just that: a fixation. Our world is in crisis—terror, injustice, alienation, environmental degradation, poverty, violence, inequality, racism, sexism—all of it. The basis for this is our cultural norm—our premier value—that for humans to be means to always be more. We are driven by an internalized imperative that says that we are nothing if we aren't trying to be more. Our culture says that being is not enough. It tells us that we can, should, and must continuously seek to develop our potential—that's what we humans are supposedly about. That's what makes us special. For example, the Earth Charter organization is a network of social and environmental activists, whose governing board includes notables like Wangari Maathai (2004 Nobel Peace Prize), Maurice Strong, and Mikhail Gorbachev. Its guiding principles are those of social justice and environmental sustainability. And its preamble states that "Fundamental changes are needed in our values, institutions, and ways of living. We must realize that when basic needs have been met, human development is primarily about being more, not having more" (Earth Charter). As this suggests people are getting the message that have all you can have is destroying the earth, but they don't want to consider that our have all you can have fixation is a result of our be all you can be obsession. It's time to rethink the entire notion of human development, and if you do, it might be the way out of your stress, insecurity, anxiety, and the awful feeling of being overwhelmed. "This is too radical," you say. Yes, it is. But it makes a lot of sense, especially if you are able to get a complete panoramic view of human history. "But even if we were satiable before, life was hard and short, and anyway, how could we ever be satiable again? What about all the modern conveniences and great technological innovations?" Fair enough, so let's not toss out the baby with the bathwater. We can be "modern" and satiable.

Why "Collective" Self-Help?

The subtitle of this book? Collective self-help. What's that? Most self-help books are very individual. They offer ways to deal with problems that may or may not have social origins or causes, but their message is, "Hey, there's nothing you can do to change forces beyond your control, but here's a way to better cope with them." If you are being swept out to sea by a riptide, there's nothing you or anyone else can do to stop it. But it would help if someone threw you a line or if you had been taught enough about riptides to know to not immediately swim against them. That knowledge and that life-line is individual self-help. This book is different. Collective self-help is about understanding your individual situation and is about explaining the real causes, so that you know what to do to eliminate them and improve your life and save yourself. Collective self-help not only explains the cause of your stress and your feeling of being overwhelmed, but shows you how to work with others who share these same feelings. Moreover, the word, collective, also points you to the solution of changing the forces around you with the help of these folks. Collective means working together to create the changes that will solve everyone's problems. Once you realize that this is what needs to happen, and you realize that with others' help it can change, you're on the road to a relaxed, sustainable future. But it's imperative to know that it does take these two pieces: 1) I've got to work with others, and 2) with their help I can actually go to the root of the problem and change the world.

With the case of the riptide, even with others' help the collective effort won't stop the tide. But here's another analogy. Suppose you need to hop in a deep swimming pool to retrieve a valuable piece of jewelry on the pool's bottom. This jewelry is not yours but belongs in your local museum. But you can't swim. You'll probably fail by yourself. But if there are enough other people sitting by the pool, they might be able to help. They'll probably be willing to help, because they feel the way you do about this jewelry. But what if none of them can swim either? You all need some collective self-help. And it's there. If all of you join hands and jump into the pool at the same time, you'll displace enough water over the pool's side to lower the water level enough to avoid drowning. It takes faith and holding hands since none can swim alone. But it can work. You have exercised some collective self-help. Of course, the others around you might need to have their minds changed about the likelihood of such an effort. But you can convince them, because they want to be convinced. They also want to see the jewelry back in the museum. Everyone gains and you've demonstrated some principles of physics. That's knowledge for a more sustainable future. It's more than technical knowledge; it's wisdom.

Another difference about the self-help in this book is that it is about real causes and explanations. Most self-help not only takes the social or economic system as a given but only looks at symptoms. These conventional self-help books don't offer explanations for root causes but only cures for the symptoms. That's not always bad. But in today's world of stress, if you don't go to the root of the problem, explain it fully, and begin from there, it's not going to make the world sustainable, and you'll only get a temporary fix. If you go to the doctor or your counseling psychologist with the complaint of stress, you're likely to get drugs or yoga for the solution. That can get you through the week, of course. But is it really what you are looking for? What you'll read here about stress and related symptoms, goes to the heart of our problems and challenges you to rethink life in ways that you've probably never considered. To say that it is collective self-help means that there are many others like you. If you begin a conversation with them—and they may be your family, coworkers, or neighbors—you are likely to discover that they, too, feel uneasy when and if they question the imperative of be all you can be.

Most of us don't ever question this notion. From our earliest memories in childhood, we have been subjected to it. It isn't actually taught to us. It is simply part of the cultural climate of our upbringing. Daniel Quinn, in his social and environmental novels, *Ishmael, My Ishmael,* and *The Story of B*, calls this social milieu, "mother culture." It says that we are *supposed* to be all we can be. What else would life be about? We don't really know where this came from, or how we came to understand its message, so we take it for granted. For one thing, all of our basic institutions operate with this assumption. What makes them function, like the economy, your family, or school, is the presumption that people go about their business with an implicit acceptance that life is about being all you can be. As a youngster, when I brought home a report card with less than perfect grades, I would be praised but with a caveat: "That's very good, but you know, you could do even better next time."

Compelled by the System

Before we go too far, there is another logical question you are no doubt asking. What about the exhilaration I feel when I learn new skills or the rush I get when I improve something and actualize some of my potential? Is this bad? Certainly not. We are not suggesting that since being is enough, we should want to discourage those who find gratification and fulfillment from being more. Even Mooch, when faced with "Be All That You Can Be" on his to-do list, remarks, "This should be intereshting." And for many it always is and for others of us, it sometimes is. The fact that we can find self-development a great thrill doesn't negate the fact that, as a cultural imperative ("Do it or feel guilty"), it is the root cause of our stress. There's more to this, as well. There is a huge difference between a world driven by this norm and a world that's not. Be all you can be is not only a personal motivation. It is what drives the society and especially the economy. How so?

The market economy, that is, capitalism, is motivated by the carrot and the stick. Essentially, if you don't enter the world and effectively compete, make something of yourself, and be all you can be *in the economic realm of life*, you are going to be left behind by those that do. You'll suffer the consequences of economic hardship, job insecurity, dead-end jobs, and low pay. Likewise, if a business doesn't try to be all it can be in the economy, then it is likely to be outcompeted and bankrupted by one that does. It is a competitive world, where individuals are on their own to sink or swim. To be successful and make it in this world, you need to pursue your self-development, actualize your potential, and keep it going for as long as you can—or for as long as you need a paycheck and some material security. Those that fail to be all they can be in the economy are likely to suffer the consequences. It's obvious. That's the stick, the motive, the incentive that makes the economy function.

People get busy when they know that the rewards go to those that achieve all they can. The carrot is that if you try to be all you can be on the job, you'll get the reward of promotion and more responsibility—which usually translates into more

autonomy and control on the job. The carrot also frequently takes the form of financial reward. If you try to be all you can be, you'll be compensated with higher
pay—so you can have all you can have. The obvious lure for both businesses and
individual workers is that having all you can have is generally a great reward for
being all you can be. It's reducible to the notion that "the good life is the goods
life." We call this consumerism, and it's a very powerful ideology.

You certainly aren't obligated to do any of this. But neither is anybody obligated to take care of you. This is an economy in which nobody owes anybody
anything. "You're on your own, pal." Your best chance is to be all you can be.
This is what drives the system. And it works pretty well, since capitalism has created more wealth in the last one hundred years than in all of our combined history.

People in the market system are compelled to be all they can be out of economic necessity. The point is that our system is driven by this, and to the extent
that you internalize this imperative and feel it is part of your inner being, then
you'll probably do just fine. Since the system drives us to be a certain way—to
be more, and furthermore, since we like the goods the system provides, we
rarely question the system. We take it for granted, because that's how we've
grown up, and it's all we know. Finally, since we don't question the system, we
don't question its be all you can be motive. We suffer the stress without knowing its cause.

But again there's a difference between your individual motivations and
those that drive the system. We need to reconsider be all you can be as the motive for the system. But as individuals we can simultaneously accept it as an
optional form of personal expression. Let's consider the idea that we should
make our economy and culture satiable systems, while freeing each of us be
more in ways that don't jeopardize others and the environment. Go ahead and
improve your golf game or your gourmet cooking, express yourself, and actualize your potential in these ways. We don't care. But let's have an economy that
doesn't require being more in order to work effectively and sustainably. Let's
reward basic responsibility on the job rather than performance.

The Be All You Can Be Culture

Our culture is a big part of the problem, too. Not only are you under economic pressure to be more and channel this effort into a productive occupation, but our culture in which capitalism is immersed, measures people by their achievements and accomplishments. For example, what if you opt out of the economic rat race? Let's say that you are in a position where you don't have to be all you can be in a career or job. You don't have to perform in order to have economic security. Maybe this is a result of inheriting some family wealth. That's fine. You don't have the stresses and insecurities that others have. If you take your leisure time, of which there will be plenty, and don't do anything with it but play, you are likely to be judged as lazy, a loser, goin' nowhere and doin' nothin'. You aren't trying to actualize your insatiable potential, in other words.

Your friends, maybe even family, and certainly acquaintances you encounter, will measure you by your achievements, or in this case, by your lack of them. If your parents and mother culture have raised you right, you'll feel guilty about this lack of interest in self-actualization. "You're not doing anything with your life." That's because you aren't behaving like a "real" human being. You're not trying to be all you can be. You don't need to, of course. There's no economic necessity for that. But if you don't use that opportunity to pursue some other form of self-development, then you'll be judged a loser. So if you're not compelled to be more, do it anyway. Learn new skills, take up art and music, get involved in civic activities. In other words, find avenues that challenge you to learn and be more. You can always spend your time trying to be a better friend, a more virtuous citizen, a more spiritual person. You are not into consumerist materialism and have all you can have, and today, many folks respect that. But mother culture says that even so, you should not let that unused human potential stay idle. It's about ambition in part. In effect, even if the object of your ambition is not money, financial success, career climbing, or occupational skill building, you should still find an outlet for your ambition. In other words, at least be ambitious with respect to something deemed socially worthy.

The idea that humans have untapped potential that's being "wasted" for lack of expression is the real issue. We treat our potential for self-actualization as the vital part of our being. For me to say that being is enough suggests that what is integral to your humanness is being wasted. That's why what you're reading here is so radical. Mother culture tells us that if people are really about developing their potential, which we realize is insatiable, then to leave any of that potential unused is a violation of our special character in the community of life. One of capitalism's strongest intellectual defenses is that it pressures us to tap this potential or else suffer the consequences. It presumably, so it goes, gives us a lot of individual freedom to express our potential in various economically-productive ways. More importantly, regardless of economic pressure, obey the Eleventh Commandment: Thou shalt not waste one's potential.

Channel your drive and talent. Ants and birds don't do this. They don't organize their lives through ambition. That's why we consider them merely survivors. They are satiable survivors. Our human ancestors, to the extent that they emulated this until the Neolithic Revolution, are generally dismissed by our modern view. What we call civilization, that is, the building up of all kinds of cultural artifacts, knowledge, technology—everything we associate with progress—is the stage in history when we are told that "real" human living began. That's when we began to think in terms of "more is better"—that simply being and living satiably is not enough. We'd otherwise be wasting our potential to improve life—our individual lives as well as that of our species and all that is linked to it. We realized, so it goes, that our special mission is to be insatiable and continuously improve ourselves and our world. Forever. However, Daniel Quinn's insight is that we moderns have failed to appreciate how successful our hunting and gathering ancestors were *without* civilization.

Without Productivism

We have become through 10,000 years of cultural evolution a species I call "productivists." We have left behind our earlier ways as survivalists, that is, the lifestyle of satiable hunters and gatherers, in favor of the insatiable lifestyle of productivism. The terms, productivist and productivism, we will be using throughout the remainder of this book. Again, the issue for us today is not whether being a productivist is a good or bad thing. It may work well for you despite the stress and feeling of being overwhelmed. It's not about good or bad or about moral versus immoral. The central issue is the degree to which you understand how the culture and economy compel you to be this way and pressure you in the direction of unrelenting stress. The logic of the system is productivism—be all you can be. What our culture values is our behavior that demonstrates ambition, drive, self-direction, achievement, accomplishments, self-actualization, self-realization, self-development, and finally, performance. This package of personality traits is what gets you ahead. Productivism is all about getting ahead.

Of course, this isn't universal, as we can appreciate the Buddhist way, too. If you insist to a Buddhist friend that life is about getting ahead, she or he will say, "Ahead of what?" You probably have an answer though: it's getting ahead of everyone else. Yet there have been and still are some cultures in which productivism is less valued than compassion, generosity, care, and kindness.

As globalization of capitalism continues to envelop the rest of the world, productivism will dominate these other values. It started in Europe with the market economy, and over the past 400 years has secularized, materialized, and now productivized all cultures it encounters. It's not that our productivist culture today rejects care and compassion. But the rewards of material security, a livable income, and social esteem tend to follow the ambitious achievers. In fact, those that maximize their self-development, usually come out on top in the competitive struggle for security. Their compensation is the accumulation of enormous wealth. Ask the world's 358 billionaires, whose combined wealth is greater than the bottom half of humanity, how they got there. They will say, "Through hard work, ambition, drive, and strive." In other words, by being a productivist, they got ahead. The successful elite, whom we generally measure by their financial success, may often be very generous and compassionate. But it is not these traits that account for their success. You already know this.

The getting ahead game is global; it rewards productivism, and it's usually our only ticket to material security. But it is a game in the sense that it is a competitive struggle: compete or die. Firms have to compete in the same way we do as workers. They have to be productivists also. The logic is pervasive, in part, because we all start this race or game with a fundamental insecurity: "you're on your own, pal." It doesn't matter whether it is a business, your business, selling your labor, or calling the shots in a big corporation. The rule is: "perform or else." You must perform or suffer the consequences. Being caring and compassionate is not going to put food on the table. It may help, but performance is the key value in the productivist world. Is there a limit to getting ahead? Is it satiable? Of course not. It's a game with no finality to it. It's never over, as there is always more potential to be actualized and more stuff to produce and consume. Is this beginning to sound like the basis for your stress? It should. When we talk about the culture and the economy from this perspective, it frequently adds up to a tidy market basket of goods on the one hand and a package of emotional strains on the other. We get them both and hope that the goodies adequately compensate for the strains of obtaining them.

Security versus Freedom

Were our pre-Neolithic ancestors productivists? No. Before the Agricultural Revolution, for about a million-and-a-half years, humans like the Neanderthalers lived successfully without it. The Neanderthalers, or *Homo erectus*, lived in southern Europe for 250,000 years as hunters and gatherers. We productivists have only been around for a few hundred years. They lived in small clans or tribes, took care of each other, and met their needs through collective and cooperative labor. It is important to appreciate the secret to their success, or what Quinn calls their "real wealth:" material security. They were motivated by the desire to assure each other security, to take care of each other. Today's culture says that it's about being all you can be. Their culture, which was totally different, said that it's about taking care of each other. And they did that.

Are we idealizing the Neanderthalers' short life without much comfort? The average lifespan was about twenty years. It was not a comfortable or convenient way to live. That's true. To get beyond your stressful life, do you and I need to live like our ancestors? No. Here's the key: we need to recognize what they did have, because it is what we need in order to live simply, justly, and harmoniously with each other and nature. What we have is a lot of individual freedom to be more and a lot of toys and conveniences that go along with it. To say that their lives lacked meaning, purpose, fulfillment, and value because they lived short tough lifestyles doesn't do them justice. Archeologists, by examining their meager artifacts, realize that there was meaning and purpose to their way. What we can learn is that life can be fulfilling and gratifying, and in fact, joyful through the exercise of collective, cooperative experience in taking care of each other. Their lesson for us today is that the emotional security our ancestors obtained by working together to produce material security is the reason for their success. It's the quality of relationships that you have with others that ultimately counts. This is what gave these folks purpose and meaning.

Security is satiable and lives organized around it are, too. The freedom to be always more is not. Our modern lives are not focused on taking care of each other. We are focused on taking care of ourselves—and in a competitive fashion. Our ancestors didn't live in order to be more. To say that material things didn't matter much to them shouldn't imply that life didn't matter to them. What we learn from both our indigenous communities today and their ancient counterparts is that what matters in life is not so much comfort but the purpose and meaning derived from a feeling of belonging, being cared for, and caring for others in a satiable and sustainable culture. What was given up when we embarked on the improvement path was what matters most in life—the feeling of collectively and mutually created security.

Did they face insecurities? Yes, but there's a difference between theirs and ours. For our hunter and gatherer ancestors the insecurity they surely faced was not individual but collective. For the tribe as a whole, we know from anthropology that they had concerns, fears, and anxieties regarding a range of uncertainties. For example, unpredictable weather would alter their usual food sources; there could be droughts and food scarcity; injuries and sickness were a source of insecurity. So at the collective level of the tribe, insecurity was a reality. But not for the individual. Each member of the group was taken care of by the others.

As long as one was part of the clan, she or he did not have to be insecure about food, clothing, and shelter. By virtue of being a member, you were taken care of. This is important because it means that their motive to work, hunt, and gather was not driven by today's logic of "you're on your own, pal." They got up and went about daily life on the basis of obligation rather than fear of starvation. The individual motive to work and participate was not the individual's fear of being left out in the cold or being a loser in a competitive struggle. Unfortunately, their presumed fear of starvation has become conventional wisdom for us. We generally believe that our ancestors were motivated by this insecurity. The point is that insecurity was not an individual motive even though it may have existed for the collective. They faced this fear together with each one knowing that she or he would be taken care of by the group, and if times became hard, they would share the hardship. This is the same for today's indigenous peoples around the world.

In our market economy it is actually fear of economic hardship or even starvation that motivates us to get up and get going day after day. Insecurity is an economic motive, the stick that drives us. Each of us is on our own, family and friends notwithstanding, to meet our material needs independently. In capitalism, insecurity is an individual motive to perform and produce. That's partly why we have become productivists. Additionally, insecurity is not a collective motive, because we assume that each individual will take care of him- or herself.

Assured or Earned Security?

Since we can state that insecurity in some form or another is basically universal to the human condition—they had it and we have it—there are really only two ways to deal with it. The first way to address insecurity is our ancestors' way: the "assured" way. The second, essentially the modern way, is the "earned" approach. Our ancestors and our indigenous neighbors use "assurance." You are assured of security by being part of the group. If you don't pull your weight on a particular day, you won't be left to starve. Your clan family will take care of you. They will ask you, what's the matter? And you will tell them that you feel sick, injured, or whatever. They and you know, as well, that when you are able, you will rejoin the hunting and gathering. You feel that as an obligation rather than as a fear. Your security is assured as they operate on the principle of taking care of each other.

But capitalism doesn't work like this. Our modern system uses insecurity as a way to get people to work. This doesn't mean that you can't get or be materially secure today. You can, but you have to earn it. It's not assured. There are or have been some exceptions, like the welfare states of Scandinavia, lifetime jobs in Japan, and other Social Democratic policies in the rest of Europe. So our economy and culture says, "If you want to get secure, go earn it." Our forebears said, "We handle our insecurity by first assuring it to each of us. If necessary, we'll address it as a group." Security is no less a vital need now than it was then. It's about how humans went about getting secure then compared to now. As humans evolved into insatiable improvers they made security contingent upon first being all one can be. For our ancestors security was the organizing principle of their lives. For us, productivism—be all you can be—is the organizing principle.

Our way is far more stressful. We are supposed to use our freedom to be more in order to earn our way to material security. Our ancestors didn't allow that kind of personal freedom, but they did assure security to each member. They generally shared the fear of hardship equally if needed. They competed with other neighboring clans, but not with each other. Today we seem to do both. That's more stress. "You're on your own, nobody's obligated to take of you, go earn it, compete or die." Go be all you can be and all will be well.

Here's an excellent contemporary example of the difference between assured and earned security: President Bush's second term started with his campaign to restructure the Social Security system. In his efforts to drum up public support for partial privatization, he announced its theme as the "ownership society." What "ownership" means is "you're on your own." His idea, and one that continues to resonate with the public, is that individuals must "own" their future and take responsibility for their own retirement. In other words, go earn your security. This is in sharp contrast to President Franklin D. Roosevelt's intention when the Social Security Act was passed in 1935. Roosevelt suggested that we might benefit from sharing the responsibility for our retirement years such that none would be destitute. The Act's original theme was to assure the security of old age by a program that put taking care of each other ahead of individualism. And at the time Roosevelt and the New Deal programs struck a very common chord with the public. Yet the tension between assuring and earning security echoes the broader mixed mind of the public about collectivity versus individualism. And we swing back and forth. Today the swing since the Reagan years has been to the right—you're on your own in the ownership society.

Cause for Personal and Social Optimism

To make your life easier and to make our world sustainable, we have to reconsider this imperative of always being more. Certainly security and freedom have to be examined, as we need to have both. The radical reforms examined in Part Four are intended to create a sustainable balance between freedom and security, and in general, we want to maximize both. Security without freedom is what our ancestors in previous civilizations practiced, but today we'd likely call this situation a prison—three meals a day and a roof over your head and that's all. But (unequal) freedom without assured security is what we are experiencing now. It's making us victims of a depersonalized competitive struggle. It's not moving us in a sustainable direction. Much of our analysis, then, is about reconciling freedom and security.

We will have to look at the heightened role that being responsible on the job and elsewhere will need to play. And we need to accompany this with a discussion of equality and social justice. Perhaps you can get secure, have equal freedom with others, live a life without unnecessary stress, and be relaxed with the knowledge that being is enough.

There are encouraging signs around us. The voluntary simplicity movement is one of them (Elgin 1993; de Graff, Wann, and Naylor 2001; YES magazine). The post-materialist movement in Europe is another (Schor 1998). What are they? Today's hippie dropouts? Not exactly. Voluntary simplicity is about choosing to live with fewer possessions. Of course, *involuntary* simplicity is essentially equivalent to being poor—the poverty we associate with deprivation and degradation. No one is advocating that we should save the world by choosing to be poor in this sense. There are conveniences—clean water, electrification, modern sanitation, and a host of other basic necessities that can be made universally available. But then there's the overconsumption that creates a treadmill of daily living. The voluntary simplicity movement and the post-materialist movement are calling attention to our ability to reduce consumption to a level that is both sustainable and stress-free.

These movements are not about dropping out but about living life more consciously with greater focus on quality—folks who have realized that the treadmill of be all you can be in order to have all you can have is not working for them anymore. They prefer to live a more minimalist lifestyle, be satiable, and reduce their stress. They are getting off of the treadmill. We call them "downshifters." It's not easy though. The frustration is frequently that practicing voluntary simplicity, living a quality life outside the rat race, and being a post-materialist is tough in a world devoted to the opposite. You can hop off of the treadmill but you are still inside the culture of insatiability. You can't drop out of the culture, only the economy.

It's hard to live simply, sustainably, slowly, and satiably in a world that's complicated, frantic, and insatiable. It's like swimming upstream. It *should* be easy. Therefore, collective self-help is necessary to reverse the stream's direction. Then you can go with the flow. But the voluntary simplicity and post-materialist movements are a vital start with tremendous potential. Tapping into these movements can offer a sense of belonging, community, a feeling of social potency, fellowship, and valuable moral support. On the other hand, much of what's encouraging is only about rejecting the have all you can have economy. This redirection is not enough if it's limited to the critique of have all you can have. This is true, as we will see, because the having more obsession is merely a manifestation of capitalist civilization's compulsive behavior about being more. Humanity is at a historical crossroads. It's time we rethink the be all you can be culture. We don't have to be more to make it work.

Part Two

You're a Victim of the System

Blame the Victim—Cure the Symptom

Notwithstanding accidents, illness, or disease, one of the more noteworthy features of American culture is the fact that if one complains about his or her "situation" and expresses a measure of discontent or despair, the response from friends and family is likely to be a variation of, "Well, deal with it. You can get on top of it somehow." Clearly, with respect to serious accidents or illness, we don't react quite as harshly. Cases abound where complaints are met with more empathy than, "Quit being a whiner." Complaining about being sick generally evokes sympathy, while voicing dissatisfaction with one's life doesn't. What we hear is, "Then do something about it." "Doing something" usually means attitude adjustment.

But attitude adjustment suggests something else: blaming the victim. Blaming the victim is a common accusation by leftists against today's conservative view that the poor, the unemployed, and those that suffer economic and social hardship should quit whining and take responsibility for their fate. The conservatives say, "If you're poor, get educated, and get busy. If you're unemployed, get a job. But whatever you do, don't blame the system, and instead, take charge of your life." Likewise, if you suffer from anxiety, stress, and feel overwhelmed, don't complain, do something that will make you feel better. It's up to you. Of course, this is a fundamental pillar of American ideology that focuses on individual initiative, personal ambition, and private responsibility.

When any of us talk about blaming the victim, the phrase isn't necessarily being used in a pejorative fashion. Blaming the victim is simply a way to say that those who suffer should be held accountable for their condition rather than pass the buck on to others or the system in which they exist. So with respect to the stresses and strains of modern life that most of us now experience, we are told to find our own solutions through various techniques, attitude adjustments, or reliance on self-help gurus, all of which leave the economic and social system as it is. It stays; we adapt. Thus fault lays with the victim and so does the responsibility. The surrounding cultural environment is innocent. And even if it is not innocent, we are to understand that there is little one can do about it.

What results is the flip side of the coin: curing the symptom. On one side we have, "blame the victim," while on the other, it's "cure the symptom." If you are the victim and the real cause of your whining is in fact the system around you, then by adjusting to it, we're curing the symptoms rather than the cause.

Where is this headed? If you are stressed, or "overstressed" as the psychologists often say, if you are frantic and anxious, feeling either guilty for not doing enough, accomplishing enough, or being ambitious enough, or going crazy by trying to do too much, it's not your fault. You are a victim of our cultural and economic system. But the mainstream around you says that you are to blame, and therefore you should deal with your circumstances. Get a better job, read some stress management self-help books, change your diet, and exercise. This is curing the symptoms. Blame the victim—the system stays intact; cure the symptoms—the system stays intact. The logical extreme? We all become contented productivists, the world churns ever onward, most likely toward destruction, and we become happy robots. The global economic system chugs relentlessly ahead, driven by the insatiable thirst for human improvement, self-actualization, and social-development. We are towed in its wake, thinking all along that there is no alternative to human insatiability and the self-help stress-relieving techniques that force our accommodation to a system no one seems to control.

This is not exactly news. It's the stuff of *Brave New World, 1984*, various sci-fi movies, and the message of some of the 20th century's best social theorists, like Herbert Marcuse, the Frankfurt School, and Jurgen Habermas. The ideology of capitalism and the "American Way" are powerful agents. Mother culture is constantly reminding us that this is the best of all possible worlds, and we should rely on our liberties and individual freedoms to overcome those personal obstacles that would otherwise make us whiners. The mainstream's message, which is essentially omnipresent, is about finding personal solutions to what are social problems. The point here is to help you understand that you are not the problem. You, and your guilt or stress, are victims of a much bigger cultural and evolutionary process. To be satisfied with stress-reducing techniques that leave the system unchallenged is curing the symptoms.

Describing Stress

Stress, in the broadest and most generic sense, is the major symptom of our be all you can be culture. The logic of our argument is essentially this: the productivist culture in which our capitalist economy—what I call the economy of insatiable improvers—is embedded, drives us to continuously be more, and to constantly get ahead for fear of being left behind or judged a loser. This makes us stressed, anxious, uneasy, and either frantic or depressed. But we are told that it is our problem, that we are not a victim, that the system is the solution, and ultimately that we should find ways and means to manage the stress, adjust to the world, and stay ahead of the game. Curing the symptom, in other words.

No one suggests that your stress is all in your head or that it is not real. There are about 50,000 entries under the word, stress, when one inserts this word on Google. In fact, it's an extremely popular, best selling topic, on Amazon.com. In that regard, Amazon has about 12,000 book titles that it displays under Stress. Yet by far the most serious and comprehensive clinical studies of stress are those done by the American Institute of Stress (AIS). Their web site (www.stress.org) states that although stress has been around forever—that it is not strictly a function of our sped-up and congested world—there is more of it today. It is more hazardous to our health today, and research has confirmed that it is intensifying other physiological problems. The term was coined by Dr. Hans Selye about forty years ago, and the Institute was founded in 1978. So what's new about stress is its magnitude.

Consequently, there is an enormous amount of data about stress that has been and continues to be collected and studied. In fact the cover story for *Time* magazine in 1983 called stress the "epidemic of the eighties," stating that it was America's number one health problem. AIS adds that stress has only worsened in the last two decades, citing survey results done in the 1980s and again in the late 1990s. They also mention that "contemporary stress tends to be more pervasive, persistent and insidious because it stems primarily from psychological rather than physical threats" (AIS). For our hunter and gatherer ancestors, stress existed as a way to stimulate humans and other animals to respond effectively under random occurrences of environmental threat. It was not an everyday feature of life.

Stress, from a more clinical explanation, is expressed by increased blood pressure, heart rate, blood sugar, breathing, muscle tension, and metabolism. It's essentially the body's reaction characterized by the "fight or flight" response (Davis, McKay, and Eshelman 2000, 2). So none of the experts consider stress to be unequivocally bad or harmful. But today most of it is, because the "stressors of life" are "unrelenting" (2). Stress has become chronic, pathological, and it frequently affects all of the body's systems. "Repeatedly invoked, it is not hard to see how they [bodily defense mechanisms] can contribute to hypertension, strokes, heart attacks, ulcers, neck or low back pain, and other 'diseases of civilization'" (AIS).

The current literature on stress, to its credit, does examine many of the environmental causes. But here we have to use the word, cause, very carefully. The discussions of the stressors of life are in many respects not the root of the problem but are further or more detailed descriptions of it. How so? For example, the National Institute of Occupational Safety and Health (NIOSH), whose surveys are widely cited, concludes that "occupational pressures and fears are far and away the leading source of stress for American adults" (AIS). They state that 40 percent of workers feel that their jobs are very or extremely stressful; a quarter say their jobs are the number one stressor in their lives; three fourths say they believe that there is more stress at work than a generation ago (AIS). Can we therefore generalize and argue that a main "cause" of stress is our jobs? In a sense, yes, but on the other hand, we need to carry this further and ask, "But why are the jobs so stressful in the first place?" What is it about work that makes it that way? Maybe stressful jobs are the "effect" of deeper problems rather than the "cause." The point is that a phenomenon can be both a cause of one thing and simultaneously the effect of something else.

NIOSH studies have also concluded that stress is due to the fact that Americans are working longer and harder than a generation ago, and we are now the most overworked labor force in the industrial world (AIS; Schor 1992). Absenteeism due to job stress has been increasing, as well. And finally, stress due to job insecurity has skyrocketed. "A 1999 government study reported that more jobs had been lost in the previous year than any other year in the last half century, and the number of workers fearful of losing their jobs had more than doubled over the past decade" (AIS). In fact, the United Nations in 1992 called work stress an international problem and "the 20th century epidemic" (AIS). In 1996 the World Health Organization stated that job stress was a "world wide epidemic." So it's not just an American phenomenon, even though it costs the U.S. $300 billion a year in lost productivity, medical costs, absenteeism, and other related expenses. This data alone suggests that at a deeper level, job stress is a function of some particular features of the global market system.

Before exploring these features, it must be mentioned that the level of analysis in the stress literature pretty much ends there. There's plenty of discussion about stress on the job due to mean-spirited bosses, tyrannical supervisors, sexual harassment, unsafe working conditions, and a host of other similar factors. In fact, a recent AIS survey found that 73 percent of American workers say that they would not want their boss's job (AIS). The findings are illuminating, but they don't go any further.

Of course, these surveys are specifically about job related stress, but there's ample evidence cited by AIS that the average American's life is not only stressful as a producer but also as a consumer, suburban commuter, and family member (de Graaf, Wann, and Naylor 2001). Stress seems to be everywhere. The stressors of life are a permanent feature of daily existence. Again, the stress literature adequately addresses such factors as the suburban rat race, the production-consumption treadmill we experience, the human congestion, time scarcity, and so on. But one is left with the impression that those are the ultimate causes, and therefore the analysis is finished and complete. But it isn't. So contemporary stress analysis is fine as far as it goes. Their findings have been scientifically validated. But that's no reason to stop digging deeper. What has happened in the literature is that with this level of examination, the self-help techniques take over.

Curing the Stress Symptoms

If you don't want to think about the deeper issues and feel compelled to start doing something about your stress, you don't have to go far. Besides the stress management and reduction classes offered in most community adult education programs, the employer-sponsored classes, and university wellness centers, there's Amazon.com. Thousands of books, audio cassettes, and videos are available. One popular seller is *The Relaxation and Stress Reduction Workbook*, now in its fifth edition with half-a-million copies sold and ranking in the top one thousand of Amazon's sales (Davis, McKay, and Eshelman 2000). It's an excellent self-help book with lots of relaxation techniques with which to experiment, all in a workbook format.

Another title is *Stress Relief and Relaxation Techniques*. Judith Lazarus, the author, suggests techniques like confiding your stress feelings in conversations with trusted friends, walking away from the stressors, taking time out, deep breathing, and yoga. This is only the tip of the technique iceberg. There's exercise, sleep, nutrition, meditation, biofeedback, guided imagery, aromatherapy, hypnosis, and hydrotherapy (Lazarus 2000). Then there's Allen Elkin's *Stress Management for Dummies*. Elkin mentions up front that we are actually "overstressed," as the problem is epidemic. "If anything characterizes our lives these days," he says, "it is an excess of change. We are in a constant state of flux. We have less control over our lives, we live with more uncertainty, and we often feel threatened, and, at times, overwhelmed" (Elkin 1999, 10). He's absolutely correct as far as he goes. But then attention turns to adjustment techniques, which is "This is how you get control, deal with uncertainty, feel less overwhelmed," and so on. It's great, but it's curing the symptoms.

When we talk about curing the symptoms of stress, it usually involves attitude adjustment, something mental that you need to do in order to cope effectively with the outside world, your job, your boss, or your two hour commute to work. Lazarus mentions Dr. Carl Hammerschlag's use of "pyschoneuroimmunology" (PNI) in his practice. Hammerschlag says that "the most critical ad-

justment people need to make in dealing with stress is to reprogram their thinking to understand that stress is not an event, but their reaction to it" (Lazarus
2000, 5). It's a fairly elegant word and surely a sophisticated technique, but it
boils down to attitude adjustment. Curing the symptoms. The world around us
continues to be the source of stress. It stays; you change. Such a technique allows you to "resist in ways that are productive rather than destructive" (1). One
of my favorite titles is *Getting Things Done: The Art of Stress-Free Productivity*
(Allen 2001). Its sales rank on Amazon is now 110—clearly a popular book.
David Allen's thesis is that stress interferes with our productivity and with the
proper techniques one can perform and produce, insatiably actualize one's potential, accomplish a lot, and self-develop with the minimum of stress. We can
be stress-free productivists, in other words. Yet if the stress you feel is actually
due to the imperative of be all you can be, if "getting things done" is the real
cause of our stress, then "stress-free productivity" is not only a contradiction but
an oxymoron. This is truly curing the symptom.

A similar example is an article I happened to notice in a recent issue of a
coffee table magazine from Pinehurst, North Carolina, the *Pinehurst Magazine*
(March 2002). The title, "Surviving Work Stress: The Good and the Bad," stated
that workplace stress is a familiar experience but a "necessary thing." "Stress
keeps us motivated, pushes us to achieve and can be the driving force behind our
successes." Again, what we can conclude is that being all you can be is *the* sin-
gle-most important thing, so stress is actually useful as a whip to keep us in the
get-ahead game. If it gets too excessive then stress can be dysfunctional, but
otherwise our conventional wisdom suggests that we must forge ahead on the
treadmill of insatiable self-development.

It's for these kinds of reasons that we have to dig deeper about causes.
Maybe the solution involves ridding ourselves, and the culture and economy that
induces it, of the need to be always productive, always having to get things
done, always having to be more tomorrow than we are today.

The self-help literature doesn't want to rock the boat. It doesn't want to say
that the system is the problem or that capitalism needs to be rethought. It especially doesn't want to undermine the cultural belief that life is about insatiable
self- and social-development. Nor does it want to subvert the imperative of being all you can be. So it contents itself with techniques that will help you live a
less stressful life all the while being as productive with your life as possible.
And we all know that being as productive with your life as possible is insatiable.
It doesn't have an end. So if you have a stress problem, it is *your* stress problem.
You are not a victim. Adjust. That's curing the symptom.

Finally, in defense of the self-help literature, there is a partial truth to it. If
you are going to go to the root of the problem, as Karl Marx suggested we do,
you have to be in a condition to think about your life in relation to the world
around you. If the stress you suffer is so extreme that it immobilizes not only
your body but your brain as well, then these techniques can get you to the point

of feeling at least functional. If your stress and frantic living, or depression, is so bad that holding a job is difficult, having decent relationships is a problem, or getting by day-to-day is next to impossible, then go for the self-help. You can't get a grip on the deeper issues or begin to try to change the world if you can't function adequately from one day to the next.

For example, if you suffer from a debilitating drug addiction that might be caused by a history of domestic violence, which itself might be due to poverty and joblessness in the family, then getting help through rehab is the first place to start. But it's only the starting point. Once you get straight then the next thing is to examine the string of causes and effects that led you to this tragic circumstance. There's a whole set of linkages that might point to a new awareness. You dig through layers of your personal history. You might find that much of what has happened had to do with the nature of the system. Maybe the poverty and unemployment had to do with capitalism. Maybe capitalism is merely an effect itself—an effect of much deeper and broader cultural forces that preceded it. That's a radical awareness. One that not only Marx, but Sigmund Freud, Albert Einstein, and Mahatma Gandhi would understand and even applaud.

The Root of the Problem: The Culture of Capitalism

A radical awareness alone doesn't count for much, of course. If we polled many of the psychologists who work with stressed-out clients, they might agree that much of the stressors of life are a result of capitalism and our culture of be all you can be. But the difference between them and some of the rest of us is that they don't make a point out of trying to change the world and are more content to offer therapeutic remedies. Still, as a victim of stress, to realize the need for social change is a good place to begin.

This realization, the radical awareness, only begins with the description of stress. To better understand it, we have to examine two interrelated spheres of modern life: capitalism and the broader culture in which it is situated. Figure 2.1, The World of Productivism I, illustrates the relationship between the two.

Figure 2.1. The World of Productivism I

The inner circle is the economic system we call capitalism. It's composed of a set of institutions that we generally take for granted: 1) the profit motive; 2) private ownership of the means of production—our businesses, their factories and offices; 3) a group of wage workers who sell their labor to the business owners; and most importantly, 4) market exchange. This is the economic system, the economy of insatiable improvers, and it is also the have all you can have economy. It is an economic system that not only knows no limits but is driven by growth, requires growth, and views growth as the only viable solution to our pressing social problems.

The outer circle is our culture. By this we mean in the broadest sense the context or terrain of meanings that we take for granted, grow up with, and assimilate as part of our being. It is what we have, or use, to make sense out of our world and find our place in life. We don't normally study our culture, learn it thematically in school, or have any of its meanings actually taught to us. It is simply the unconscious ground that allows us to go about our daily activities and also plan our futures—Quinn's mother culture. So capitalism exists and is embedded within a particular type of culture, what I call the culture of insatiable freedom—the be all you can be culture. You can't understand capitalism without seeing it as an effect of the bigger culture around it, in other words. From this perspective, capitalism is both a cause and an effect. Of course, to the extent that capitalism functions properly, it reinforces the culture, and likewise with the culture—to the extent that people accept be all you can be and put a premium on their individual freedom, capitalism is reinforced. The totality of all of this we call the World of Productivism.

First, why do we call capitalism both the economy of insatiable improvers and the have all you can have system? What is it about this economy that makes it a cause of our stress, anxiety, and feeling of being overwhelmed? It's a fairly short story because capitalism, the market economy, hasn't been around very long. It emerged in the 16th century in Europe. Before capitalism and in many regions of the world, there were markets, the use of money, trade, and prices—the mechanisms we associate with capitalism. But there was no capitalism because none of the precapitalist societies depended on exchanging goods and services in markets to meet basic material needs. So with capitalism a "great transformation" occurred, as the Hungarian economist, Karl Polanyi emphasized (Polanyi [1944] 1957). People in Europe went from having very little freedom to pursue their economic self-interest and very little dependence on selling things in markets, to precisely the opposite: lots of individual freedom to get ahead and total reliance on market exchange to get needs met.

Such an economic system had never before been tried. In fact, our experience with it is still quite in doubt even though we are led to believe by modern culture that it has been around for an eternity. Our earliest human ancestors, *Homo erectus*, evolved in Africa and began their migration outward over a million years ago. Consequently, as a fraction of our human history, capitalism represents about 0.05 percent. The next wave out of Africa was our most direct lineage: *Homo sapiens*. They left on their hunting and gathering journey about one hundred thousand years ago. In that case, capitalism is 0.5 percent of our experience. Next, about ten thousand years ago, *Homo sapiens*, settled down in a few places—only a few—and became self-sufficient farmers and built up civilizations. That makes capitalism merely 5 percent of our civilized experience. Not much in any of these cases. No wonder Polanyi referred to capitalism's emergence as the great transformation. Our history is far richer in hunting and gathering and self-sufficient agriculture than it is with economic self-interest and market exchange. And our knowledge of how it works is still in its infancy even though the system seems mature. It is such a powerhouse of growth and technological change that it gives the appearance of being our only economic experience. In fact, in the last half-century humans have produced more goods and services—output—than all of humanity combined in all of previous history!

What Drives Capitalism?

There are three forces that drive capitalism: insecurity, individual freedom, and competition. When these are combined we get the dynamic, innovative, wealth-producing juggernaut of insatiable improvement. First, we have to explain how insecurity and personal freedom to get ahead work together to create capitalism's dynamic of growth. Capitalism emerged from what Polanyi called embedded economies. These were the village, slave, or feudal systems that existed all over the world prior to the 16th century. They had one thing in common: economic behavior was highly controlled or governed by social norms, customs, and traditions. There was little freedom to pursue one's individual economic self-interest, and work was motivated by obligation and command. The purpose of economic activity was quite different, too. People viewed taking care of each other as the primary purpose. And even though the group, the tribe, or the village might be insecure, the individual was taken care of. His or her security was assured as a result of being a member of such little societies.

With capitalism all of that changes. The operative term becomes, "You're on your own, pal." The individual was unleashed from the constraints of the group. In Europe, the serfs who had been tied to the land, were freed to search for other employment. And in fact, they were often forced to leave the land—were evicted—as the aristocracy enclosed the common lands with fences to graze sheep for the burgeoning textile industry. They became the propertyless, mobile labor force that ultimately constituted the wage workers of the Industrial Revolution.

With capitalism then insecurity becomes the fundamental whip. Unlike its predecessors, capitalism obligates no one to take care of you. It's a sink or swim situation. But the upside is that you are now free to get ahead, go out into the market and realize your most promising options.

But it is a market economy where all needs are met by exchanging something. This is an imperative that becomes a motivator along with insecurity. "Sell something or die" is the condition. Businesses have products and services to sell and workers have their labor to sell. As long as everyone has something to sell that others want to buy, and as long as others have money to buy things, then it works.

So whether we are talking about landless wage workers or crafty business owners, they are both in the same boat when it comes to the imperative to sell. The entire system rises and falls with market exchanges. If you don't spend your income, the firm doesn't make the anticipated sales; they don't hire the workers so workers don't get jobs, and they don't have income to spend on the firms' goods. The system begins to implode, and that's a recession or depression, if things fall far enough. Nothing you didn't already know.

Consequently, everybody in capitalism starts out with a kind of existential insecurity but also with the freedom to deal with it—as individuals. Businesses feel insecure because they can't be sure that there will be buyers for their output at profitable prices. Workers are insecure because they can't be sure that firms will find it profitable to hire them at livable wages. But what saves the system is the freedom that everyone presumably has to earn their security. Firms have the freedom to innovate, find new markets, change prices, and so on. Workers have the freedom (although not equally so) to relocate to perhaps more promising industries, get more education, or save their paychecks and start their own businesses. Everyone can be entrepreneurial, so the ideology goes. Thus, insecurity is handled by exercising one's freedom and earning it in the market. Even though insecurity is not new, earning it rather than collectively assuring it is. As Jeremy Rifkin points out, "If we just provide everyone with the opportunity to go to school, allow the free market to rule, and make sure the government doesn't interfere too much in its workings, the motivated and talented will rise to the top on their own accord. And those that aren't motivated and/or lack talent will not do well—but that's the nature of things" (Rifkin 2004, 40).

Precapitalist societies, regardless of their class structure, their tribal character, or their hunting and gathering, provided security at the expense of freedom. Capitalism reverses this. Freedom is purchased at the expense of security. If there was little freedom to earn our way out of it, the system would have been overthrown long ago. At the same time, the carrot that operates with the stick is the reward of either big profits or a better job.

But insecurity and individual freedom are not the only forces. Competition is the remaining element that intensifies our fundamental insecurity. If insecurity is what tosses us into the river of sink or swim, it is competition that moves us downstream. It is not enough to simply tread water. The market system, with production for exchange, drives us downstream because if we don't compete, we'll be a loser. After all, this is a system of compete or die. Firms are insecure, in part, because they have to compete with other firms, and if competition, that is, free trade, is sufficient the firm has little control over prices and market share. According to the conservative theory (neoclassical theory as it is called in economic circles), the firm in a pure/perfect competition market has control over how much to supply in the market but nothing else. The price is determined in the market competitive process through the interaction of supply and demand. The "impersonal forces of the market" rule—competition rules, that is. If the price is too high and there is excess supply, then competing firms drive it down. If the price is too low and there is excess demand, competing consumers drive it upward. The equilibrium price that results is the byproduct of a circumstance in which firms are price takers rather than price makers. In such markets, the firms are themselves victims of a competitive condition in which they are ruled by forces that no one in particular controls. They are subordinated to the "laws of the market"—everyone in general but no one in particular controls. "You are at the mercy of the market," as the saying goes.

Likewise with labor markets and workers. If there are competitive labor markets then each worker is also at the mercy of the market. Workers compete with each other for jobs, and if wages are too high, firms hire fewer employees, and a surplus of labor exists—that's unemployment. Workers compete with each other for a scarcity of jobs and drive down wages. Wages, just like prices of goods, go up and down based upon the competitive forces of supply and demand. Ultimately, the going wage is determined by forces external to the individual worker—or firm, for that matter.

In capitalism every player is at the mercy of the market, workers' incomes based on wage rates and business's incomes based on profits, are largely the outcome of competitive forces. In the pursuit of their economic self-interest, competition is supposed to give workers a livable wage according to how productive they are, consumers are supposed to get the most products for the lowest possible price, and firms are expected to make no more than the minimum amount of profit to keep them in business. This is what the founding father of economics, Adam Smith, called the invisible hand of the market—self-interest furthers the general interest, and basic needs are met through competition, the whip of insecurity, and the exercise of individual freedom.

No wonder everyone in capitalist society is nervous or stressed—insecurity is fundamental to the system. And no one likes the insecurity, even though they embrace the freedom. No one likes the competition. This much is certain. What we've witnessed over the past two hundred years of capitalism is the continuous efforts by both workers and firms to avoid competition in any way they can. Workers try to form unions or get protection in the form of unemployment compensation or minimum wage legislation. Firms try their best to create monopolies, drive out the competition, and also get protective legislation like patents and copyrights. Although competition is basic to the structure of capitalism and an ideological pillar, no one wants to submit to it. Why? Because competition leaves little room for control and a lot of room for insecurity. One's best bet is the effective exercise of freedom to find ways to either eliminate the competition or be a better competitor. No wonder people feel victimized by the system. No wonder stress is rampant.

Insatiable Improvement

Surviving the compete-or-die, sink-or-swim, insecure market jungle of capitalism is clearly possible. How so? On the basis of a specific individual freedom: be all you can be. Be a productivist. Get motivated, accomplish things, be self-directed, be ambitious, achieve all you can. Scan the economic horizon for new ways to get ahead, innovate, get skilled, and in fact, overachieve. You can be a winner. Don't let stress get in your way either.

This is the notion of insatiable improvement. It applies to businesses as well as to workers. The ticket to success is continuous improvement. The more any of the players pursue improvement of skills, decision making, technology, learning, talents, and competencies, the more probable is their success, the less insecurity they will have, and the more control they'll experience. It sounds stressful because it is.

It's essentially about self- and social-development. It's about organizational development and personal development. It applies at all levels of economic activity, from firms motivated by profit, to nonprofits desiring more influence or the advancement of their cause, to workers wanting a decent standard of living, to politicians, churches, and school kids wanting to succeed. Improvement and development is the same thing. We don't talk about development except for the assumption that it contributes to improving life or anything deemed good that connects with human existence. Capitalism mandates the condition of "improve or die" and "develop or die," partly because it is a compete-or-die system. It's a competitive struggle. And it's coercive. The trick is to make people insecure, give them individual freedom, make them compete and then watch how they scramble to develop and improve everything they can. Businesses are driven to it; workers are driven to it, and pretty much everyone else is, too.

This is not an economic system that knows limits. Because it is a competitive situation, and because humans seem capable of endless self- and social-actualization of their potential, to ask, "How much is enough?" is irrelevant. Are there limits to economic growth since we are now facing the reality of limited carrying capacity of the earth's biosphere?

The message that you can't have infinite growth on a finite planet is finally getting through to us—maybe. As Daniel Quinn's character, Ishmael, states, "You're captives of a civilizational system that more or less compels you to go on destroying the world in order to live" (Quinn 1992, 25). Although Ishmael is alluding to the environmental crises resulting from economic growth, the question is, "What's the compulsion behind the growth?" It's the fact that continuous expansion is built into the structure of the system itself. We have unlimited growth that has now become both uneconomic and destructive in part because the competitive forces of the market compel all the players to insatiably improve and develop. But improvement and development is not the same thing as economic growth. The coercive drive for improvement and development generally results in more economic growth, and we are only now beginning to see the social and environmental consequences of limitless growth. But we haven't let go of the old saw that "there's always room for improvement." As much as some are ready to reel in the growth, no one is talking about rethinking insatiable improvement and development.

Performance Stress? What's It Get You?

The ideology of capitalism has never suggested that the purpose of the system is to create social justice, equality, love, relaxation, tranquility, or any other lofty values. There are two paramount icons of its ideology: personal freedom and lots of material goods, that is, wealth. We've examined the issue of individual freedom and its link to insecurity, but what about wealth? The massive accumulation of wealth that capitalism creates can't be debated. The global economy's output expands as much in each year now as it did in an entire century before 1900 (Ayres 1999, 39). Its purpose is largely reducible to this: it's a wealth-producing machine. So along with the mantra of maximizing human freedom, the other ideological pillar is that "the goods life is the good life"—consumerism. What's the system about? Delivering the goods. What's modern living about? Shop 'til you drop, happiness-through-buying, and ultimately, have all you can have.

The be all you can be performance side of the economy is directly related to the have all you can have consumer side of it. As Figure 2.2 indicates they are mutually reinforcing mechanisms that together power the system. They work in tandem to pump out lots of stuff and create mammoth improvements. People and organizations are driven to actualize their potential, be always more and have always more, yet the overburden from all of this are stress and anxiety.

Figure 2.2. The World of Productivism II

**Product Markets
Consumerism
*Have All You Can Have***

CAPITALISM

**Factor Markets
Performism
*Be All You Can Be***

The diagram illustrates the basic workings of the market system. There are factor markets where various kinds of labor are exchanged, and there are product markets where goods and services are bought and sold. Essentially, people sell their labor to firms in the factor markets and take their wages and salaries and enter the product markets where they spend their incomes on the stuff they helped to produce. This is called the circular flow diagram in text book economics. The twist in this particular case is that we focus on workers' performance while under the employ of firms in the factor markets, and then their consumerism in the product markets.

Yet whether one is a wage worker or business owner, performance matters. The firm is under competitive pressure to perform and produce as efficiently as possible all of the time, and so is the worker. This amounts to the compulsion to be all you can be, actualize your potential, develop skills and competencies, produce, accomplish, achieve, and be ambitious. These are the values of what we call performism. Perform or die is the rule in this case. It applies to both the firm owners and their employees.

But there's a payoff and reward on the consumer side: to compensate for the stress of being all you can be and performing to the max, you can have all you can have. The more you perform, the more income, profits, and salaries you get, then the more you can buy and actualize the "American Dream." In other words, to have all you can have, you have to be all you can be. On the other hand, the reward for being more tomorrow than you (or your business) are today, is being able to have more tomorrow than today. Being more on the job gets you more stuff on the market. The incentive system works this way.

For a firm's successful performance—that is, its efficient production—it gets more profits. The owners and stockholders have more income to spend on all kinds of great commodities, luxuries, and treats. For workers, the harder they work and more productive they are, the higher their pay and the more stuff they can have, as well. Performance gets rewarded with consumerism. More consumerism requires more performance. And around and around it goes with no end in sight and none desired. This system has worked pretty well, except for periods like the 1930s Depression in the United States and elsewhere. Americans, after World War I, embraced the idea that the goods life is the good life, and businesses were happy to comply. The stress of having to perform and be all you can be was partially offset by the thrill of feasting at the smorgasbord of consumer choice—have all you can have.

This mutual reinforcement has a condition attached to it, however: workers need to accept the idea that buying things is a fair trade for putting up with meaningless or demeaning jobs. In other words, what happened in the 1920s was a conscious shift from finding gratification in work to finding it in consumption (Ewen and Ewen 1982, Ewen 1976). The American labor force basically traded off the demand for participatory, empowering, and meaningful experience on the job for higher incomes that would fetch them more material goods and a higher level of consumption. They accepted the reality of alienated labor that Marx analyzed in return for more money and a higher standard of living. Not much has changed since then.

The performism-consumerism circle is still primarily an economic phenomenon that lies within the inner circle of Figure 2.1. The culture of insatiable freedom and be all you can be, the outer circle, is The World of Productivism that we have yet to fully reveal.

Affluenza: The Stress of Have All You Can Have

One factor that compounds the stress and anxiety of modern living is the fact that neither is limited to the performance side of the economy. There's consumption stress, too. This has been given a clinical name: affluenza (de Graaf, Wann, and Naylor 2001). *Affluenza* is a delightful book that is actually a result of the popular PBS movie by the same title. NPR's Scott Simon, who hosted the television version of *Affluenza*, stated that the show "aired in the late 1990s, a time when more Americans were feeling fatter bank accounts—and more hollowness inside. Shopping and stock market speculation were becoming the genuine national pastimes. But at the same time, greater numbers of Americans were seeking to cash themselves out of what was becoming to them a daily rough-and-tumble struggle for mere things" (de Graaf, Wann, and Naylor 2001, ix). Affluenza is described as *the* disease of consumerism—pathological buying and shopping—that results in a lifestyle on the "work-and-spend treadmill" (Schor 2004, 1998, 1992). It's really "overconsumption" that's at issue.

What are the symptoms of affluenza? They follow in part from what Jeremy Rifkin calls "hypercapitalism," the "hypercommercial environment" of today's global capitalist system (Rifkin 2000). He says that "the interval between desire and gratification is quickly approaching simultaneity as consumers come to expect a greater array of novel products and services at near breakneck speed" (22). Mark Hertsgaard adds

> Some of us find it exhausting to live in a society where time seems always to be speeding up, where every new gadget—e-mail, cell phones, Palm Pilots—promises us more freedom and convenience but also further separates us from the larger community and our inner selves. We complain about stress (and gobble $800 million worth of drugs a year to compensate), we resent not having enough time with our kids, we can be nostalgic for our rural past and its calmer ways. But in the end, we are creatures of society, and we can neither recognize the full damage being done to us nor see any real alternative (Hertsgaard 2002, 118).

Bottom line symptoms, then, include such stressors as "possession overload"—where our toys control us rather than us controlling them, "time famine," alienation from our friends and family, and "chronic congestion." Remarkably, the self-storage industry occupies over a billion square feet and is a $12 billion industry—more than the U.S. music industry (de Graaf, Wann, and Naylor 2001, 32). And we spend more on jewelry, shoes, and watches ($80 billion/year) than we do on higher education ($65 billion/year).

Then there are all of the stress symptoms related to bankruptcies, family dysfunction—"family convulsions," "keeping up with the Joneses," and the frantic rat race of trying to get up, fix the kids breakfast (and lunches), get the car gassed, make it to work on time, deal with the bosses, jet out after work, stop at the grocery store, fix dinner, do the laundry, and finally collapse into bed. It's the "daily grind." Being a performer and being a consumer in the car-dominated, suburban sprawl world, trying to keep it all together, and rise above it is surely stress and anxiety provoking. Additionally, there are a host of factors that can aggravate the whole nightmare, as well: if you're a single parent, worried about being downsized or outsourced, or your kids are in rehab or jail, or you're poor and working several jobs. The list goes on.

The point? When our high mass consumption lifestyle creates stress from having to be all we can be, we don't necessarily overcome it by being rewarded with have all you can have. *Utne* magazine, like the *Time* issue two decades earlier, also ran a special issue in 2003 that headlined, "How to Stop Time: Rip up your schedule and take back your life" (Jan.-Feb. 2003)

> On the job, in school, at home increasing numbers of North Americans are virtual slaves to their schedules. Some of what fills our days are onerous obligations, some are wonderful opportunities, and most fall in between, but taken together they add up to too much. Too much to do, too many places to be, too many things happening too fast, all mapped out for us in precise quarter-hour allotments on our palm pilots or day planners. We are not leading our lives, but merely following a dizzying timetable of duties, commitments, demands, and options (Walljasper 2003, 62).

Living itself, whether it's production or consumption, can easily become overwhelming.

Wage versus Career Labor

Finding a way out of the morass of modernism, even with the best stress relievers, self-help techniques, therapy, or by slowing down and scheduling less, is not easy, as we know. As the American Institute of Stress and the National Institute of Occupational Safety and Health are quick to point out, much of our stress is work related. And there are a variety of avenues open to us to grope our way toward less stressful jobs.

One way concerns the differences between wage labor and what I call career labor. With the beginning of capitalism, and especially the Industrial Revolution, what was commonly labeled wage labor was, in fact as Marx and other socialists understood it to be: alienated labor. As a worker, when one entered the factory in 1850, democratic decision making ended. You did as you were told. Your time on the job belonged to the company, and, more importantly, you lost control over much of the work process. Even feudal serfs had more control over their labor than factory workers. But this "alienation" of one's control over the working day, wage rates, and essentially all relevant decisions about production has been a basic feature of the capitalist landscape for two hundred years (Braverman 1974). The acceptance of alienated labor was in part due to the notion of *quid pro quo*: a fair day's wage for a fair day's labor. They control my labor, in other words, but I receive a wage in return. So be it.

If one was dissatisfied with such conditions, our neoclassical economic ideology—still very important today—suggests that the worker make good use of his or her freedom, save money, and invest it in self-employment or an entrepreneurial enterprise. In other words, you can escape the drudgery of alienated labor by being all you can be, showing initiative, and finding your own solution. Save those pennies, get a business, become a farmer, butcher, baker, or computer software maker. Not much has changed really. Having one's own business is certainly an option that many continue to aspire to, and for the same reason—to escape wage labor.

The interesting thing about alienated labor is that no one actually expects you to identify with the job, see it as your special joy, or meaningful activity. It's not a career. Bosses realize that this kind of work is alienating. They don't figure that you enjoy it much and would be shocked if you came to work full of vigor and enthusiasm. What worries them is that we might have a tendency to "soldier" on the job, that is, try to get away with doing as little as possible. Our productivity—or lack of it—concerns them. They and everyone else knows that when people hate their jobs, their productivity suffers. And if productivity suffers, so do profits. What to do? Industrial history suggests that firms do whatever is cost-effective to limit wage labor to activities that can be easily monitored for productivity. In which case, if you aren't working up to speed, the managers can tell, because they can observe your level of output and productivity. The assembly line has been an effective tool for policing productivity since industrialism's inception. In sweatshops today, particularly in the footwear and garment industries in places like Indonesia or Saipan, production quotas are common and floor supervisors pace the aisles and workstations scanning for slackers.

The stress of alienated labor can be lessened by demonstrating enthusiasm in certain cases. One can seek a promotion by showing good cheer and working harder than others. That's an escape of sorts. Also with such performance and productivist behavior, one might obtain a pay increase—the reward of increased consumerism and have all you can have. None of these options necessarily reduce job stress, but they can make us feel better, none the less.

Cleary the most significant development in the workplace in the last century has been the dramatic expansion of career labor. In fact 19th century industrialism's hallmark was manufacturing and the assembly line. Its icon was the factory. But it's been a different world for the last four decades. As we know, the United States has deindustrialized since the early 1980s, and we've witnessed a dramatic decrease in blue-collar, unionized jobs as employment has shifted to high technology and the service industry (Bluestone and Harrison 1988, 1982).

The factory is no longer the icon of industrial capitalism in the United States. As early as 1974, the social theorist Daniel Bell, predicted the coming of "post-industrial society" (Bell 1976). Since then we've witnessed corporate restructuring, downsizing, outsourcing, paper entrepreneurialism, the casino society, flexible specialization, niche marketing, just-in-time production, vertical disintegration, supply-chain management, total quality management, rightsizing, and managerial rationalization—all of which is either directed to or by one event: the securing of the U.S. post-World War II Empire in the era of corporate globalization. U.S. businesses made their deliberate competitive comeback in the late 1980s and 1990s. The capitalist economy today is in certain respects quite different than that of the post-World War II period. By 2000 "Globalization of production was no longer supplementing domestic manufacture, but replacing it" (Bluestone and Harrison 1988, 28). Manufacturing has seen a continuous decline, in fact, since the end of World War II. By the late 1980s it accounted for only 19 percent of employment and Gross Domestic Product. And the numbers have continued to decline over the past decade. The jobs created in the 1990s high tech boom were, of course, lower paying, many part-time, non-unionized, and in the service industries.

Notwithstanding the massive job loss presided over by the first Bush administration between 2000 and 2004, where both career and wage labor took serious hits, we aren't likely to see the factory icon in U.S. business's future. George W. Bush took the reins for a second term with the nefarious legacy of 900,000 fewer U.S. jobs than in 2000. Although traditional, alienated wage labor is less linked to manufacturing, it exists in the service industries today, as plenty of us know through personal experience.

But the less discussed and examined change is career labor. The high tech service economy has created millions of jobs that have a unique character: productivity is hard to measure. This is one of the defining features of career labor. When productivity is easily monitored, there's little need on the employers' part to insist that the worker embrace his or her work, demonstrate their enthusiasm, or "buy in" to it. All that matters is that workers do their job. Their attitude about it is of less concern to the bosses, because if the employee fails to produce, their low productivity will be quickly discovered, and he or she can be easily fired. Done.

But when there is a growing proliferation of jobs where it's difficult to measure one's output—managerial labor of one sort or another, service provisioning, office and clerical work—supervisors can't tell just how much "work" is getting done. What becomes pivotal in these cases is attitude. If as a boss, you can't actually measure the productivity of an office staff, to be sure that they are working as productively as possible, as efficiently as possible, and as hard as possible, you had better do an attitude check before they are hired and continuously while they are on the job. Morale, in other words, becomes important. But it's more than a morale issue.

Career labor is essentially that kind of work where the demonstration of productivist values is the critical feature. Generally, these jobs are ones in which it is not only hard to measure productivity, but they also come with more responsibility. One is paid more, because there are more demands that involve overseeing tasks, coordinating programs, initiating projects, accessing and networking clients, researching market potential, brainstorming, planning events, and of course, managing people and projects. Many of the careerist occupations require good communication skills and interpersonal networking skills. They are "people" jobs, customer relations, and marketing oriented.

Because it is hard to tell if people are working efficiently, what the employer wants to hear and see demonstrated is a set of performance values that include being self-directed, enthused, focused, ambitious, goal-oriented, achievement-driven, excited and interested in the work, and most importantly, a believer in the "mission" and "vision" of the business.

What your boss hopes to hear from you is, "I have always wanted to do this kind of work. I'm totally into this company. In fact, I want to be all I can be, and do it through this career—this job. Money is not the issue. Self-actualization is where it's at for me." Naturally, they would like to hear that from their wage workers. But they don't expect it. However, from employees who are given more responsibility and higher remuneration and whose productivity is not measurable, they demand it. If you want to get and keep a career job, you need to know and profess the litany of productivism. The key message is this: tell them and convince them that you want to be all you can be—which we and your superiors all realize is insatiable—and actualize your potential *through* your career with them.

Profess and demonstrate productivist values. That's the essence of career labor. And that can be hard work and stressful. But they will trust you with the bigger paycheck and the responsibility that accompanies it. Would you give a prospective employee such a job if they acted like it was merely a paycheck, a means to an end, and something they are not excited about? Of course not. If you suspect that they will slack, given their attitude, you're probably right. And if they do, you're not necessarily able to tell. Such things don't help profits. But it's not just profits. Those who look for work in nonprofits and various other organizations that might be charitable, movement, or cause-based, must also demonstrate productivist values. They are driven by fund raising requirements, campaign promotion, membership expansion, and so on, and they don't want an employee who doesn't care about their mission or their cause. They don't want to settle for the typical, alienated, wage-worker attitude either.

Career labor is also about commitment to the goals of the organization. Yet to demonstrate this, one must profess productivism. In Figure 2.2, this is called performism. It's a dogma, a litany of beliefs that convinces others—teachers, parents, authorities of all kinds, and bosses—that you are an insatiable self-actualizer. Essentially you must identify with their goals, but the heart of your message must be that you believe, embrace, and identify with one vital human value: the purpose of a human being is to insatiably develop her- or himself. The organization says it is into one thing: improvement and development of itself. For a career job, you must echo this as well.

You can escape the degradation of alienated wage labor by finding a career. These opportunities continue to increase as globalization and high tech production progress. Yet the downside is that attitude becomes critical. Playing the game of demonstrating productivist values can be exhausting and stressful. The more able you are to find that one niche where you really do believe in the job and organization, the easier things are, of course. No wonder a career self-help manual like *What Color Is Your Parachute?* is in its twenty-second edition. Its author cautions that "with so many unemployed people, many employers have new and higher standards for employee performance, and if you don't measure up, there are plenty of others they can find to take your place" (Bolles 1994, 12).

The career path is so vital today that we hear of endless "career fairs" and "career days" throughout America's public school systems, its colleges and universities, through magazines, and local newspapers. While visiting family in Iowa, I noticed that *The Des Moines Register* has a Sunday supplement devoted to "Business and Career," with self-help articles and book reviews that assist readers in finding their niches. One article, "Pursue your ideal career," began with, "Remember when you were a child and people asked what you wanted to be when you grew up? Have you figured it out yet?" (Kersten 2002, D1). In our culture one is never too young to begin worrying about a career, of course.

The stress starts earlier and earlier, and it is never too soon to initiate children into the culture of performance and self-development. I realized this thirty-five years ago, when student teaching first grade at an elementary school in Colorado. It took about three weeks to realize that most of what I was teaching was productivitst values: "sit down and focus on your work;" "that's good but you can do a bit better next time;" "just stay with it;" "show a little enthusiasm." It's also routine with parents and their kids. But cultural norms are assimilated in this way.

Demonstrating productivism is frequently woven into the compete-or-die fabric. You have to do it to get the job and continue it to keep it. The bottom line is that this is a performance-driven economy. It is an imperative for workers, just as it is for businesses and organizations of all kinds. Perform or die. If you have any doubts about the extent to which this is true, take a look at James Collins and Jerry Porras' *Built to Last* (1994). It's had over seventy printings, has been translated into seventeen languages, and was on the *Business Week* best-seller list for fifty-five months (Collins 2000, 135). Their message is well documented by CEOs and successful companies: success is being all you can be.

On the lighter side, check out Jennifer Aniston's quandary in the Hollywood movie, *Office Space*. Her boss at the restaurant where she waited tables was concerned that she was not sufficiently demonstrating her productivism—her "flair" was inadequate. A parody about productivism? Surely. But one of my students who saw the movie had recently been hired by the popular chain restaurant, Red Lobster. During her orientation she was given a corporate booklet that reviewed the Red Lobster mission. She was asked to recite parts of the booklet everyday to her supervisors before her shift began. She brought me a copy of it: "Our Compass." Under the heading of employee "Performance" there's "Quality: An attitude and way of doing things that is anchored in our principles combined with a relentless drive to improve, innovate, achieve, and dominate." Employees must also have "Zip: Being active, competitive, and positive." And finally, they must have "Balance: Is Red Lobster stronger because of what I did today?" Their customers are to be treated as "a treasured friend" since "the magic starts when you drive on to our parking lot." Like Jennifer Aniston, I think she quit shortly thereafter.

Yet in Collins and Porras' words, a successful organization besides having vision "must also have an unrelenting drive for progress" (Collins and Porras 1994, 216). The drive for progress is reducible to be all you can be. "Progress" is merely another way to talk about insatiable improvement and development. Mission statements are revealing in this respect. Whether or not they are actualized, they are essentially about professing productivism, because that's what people want to hear. The mission statement in my department, surely typical of most, says, "We support efforts to continuously improve the learning process by pursuing excellence in intellectual activities that enhance and advance knowledge." This is our culture. The "unrelenting drive" gives the appearance of being built into the core of our being. How could *being* ever be enough?

The Culture of Insatiable Freedom

To this point we've been examining the small circle—capitalism—illustrated in Figure 2.1, and within it, the circle of consumerism and performism in Figure 2.2. Figure 2.3 combines these.

Figure 2.3. The World of Productivism III

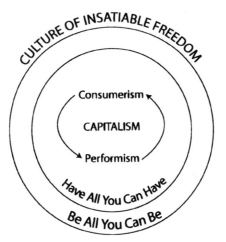

To further understand your stress and anxiety it is not enough to limit the analysis to capitalism and the inner circle. Capitalism, the economy of insatiable improvers, besides being a cause, is also an effect. It didn't originate in a cultural vacuum. In many respects it is simply an outgrowth of the historic evolution of a very unique culture: insatiable freedom. Why freedom? In all previous societies, whether or not they were civilizations; indigenous hunters and gatherers; self-sufficient, village gardeners; nomadic herders; or migratory gardeners, their ways were wildly diverse, but they all had one feature in common: taking care of each other. Their cultures were about security and assuring this to each member. Their lives were motivated, their norms and customs were situated, and their obligations were focused on taking care of each other. It is this simple anthropological fact that distinguishes all of humanity before capitalism. In *Beyond Civilization*, Daniel Quinn says, "Undoubtedly the greatest benefit of the ethnic tribal life is that it provides its members cradle-to-grave security" (150). Such security is "a true measure of their wealth."

Quinn is specifically referring to peoples who were not in civilizations. What about life in the handful of civilizations that sprouted initially in the Middle East, Northern China, and the Indus River Valley? Then more civilizations sprouted, as well. To be clear, we shouldn't say that civilizations "spread." They didn't. They were uniquely situated. According to Jeremy Rifkin, "Civilizations are a rare phenomenon in world history" (Rifkin 2002, 53). Citing Arnold Toynbee, he suggests that at most there have only been about thirty. Some scholars argue more conservatively that there have been between eight and fifteen. But even the cultures of these sedentary, class societies were about security. We can say it this way: they were more organized and oriented around taking care of each other than they were about pursuing individual freedom. In fact the individual and what we refer to as the "self" were slow to emerge and didn't count for much. The group, the tribe, or the collective is what mattered most.

For all intents and purposes there have only ever been two types of culture—that is, culture considered in its broadest fashion. The first and most pervasive is the culture of security. Then with the "great transformation" and the emergence of science, the Enlightenment, and capitalism, we witness the culture of freedom—insatiable freedom. So not only is capitalism new but the culture that surrounds and embeds it is new, too. Today, freedom is how people experience life, as well as how they organize and make sense out of it. It's not that security is unimportant, but it has been subordinated to the principle that the individual is free to be all he or she can be—to make the most or the least of his or her life. This is a culture that says not only are you "on your own," but you are free to be more tomorrow than you are today. Our lives today are not driven by the obligation to take care of each other but by the freedom to always make more of our selves.

We are not suggesting that everyone is equally free. They aren't. Some, by virtue of talent, wealth, family inheritance, race, religion, or ethnicity, face less discrimination, fewer obstacles, more privilege, and so on. They are the lucky ones who happen to be on the top of the social pyramids of their societies. They have more choices, more access to opportunities to self-actualize and get ahead, and are less the victims of social injustice than those at the bottom. The argument that life today is about individual freedom says nothing about freedom's distribution. There is tremendous inequality, and it's getting worse, as we know. But such developments don't negate the principal role of freedom in our world.

Karl Marx thought that people experienced capitalism as exploitation and injustice. And to his credit, that was a legitimate observation in the mid-19th century. But on closer examination, the ideology of personal freedom resonates much deeper and at the experiential level. By "experience," we also mean at the pre-reflective level of consciousness. Surely, as many sweatshop workers and wage laborers of all sorts in the global economy know, when they reflect and analyze their situations they feel the exploitation, degradation, alienation, and injustice punctuating their lives. Women feel patriarchal domination and/or religious and ethnic discrimination. And there are other victims of domination and oppression. But the way the culture operates is much more at the pre-reflective level of experience. It's mother culture's strongest message: "you are free to be more, to insatiably actualize your potential, to make something of yourself." Life in our culture is fundamentally about "making something of your Self."

The freedom culture not only tells people to exercise it, but also informs those who don't have much of it to fight to get it. One of the most radical, if not *the* most radical idea of our time is that of equal freedom—democracy. Most of the social justice movements of the past two hundred years have made their appeal on the basis of this principle. The U.S. civil rights movement, the women's movement, the anti-apartheid movement in South Africa—these are only a handful of such democratic movements. The notion of having an "equal say" in the decisions that affect one's life is essentially about the idea of an equal access to the pursuit of individual freedom. The point is that the idea of freedom is not simply a common feature of all industrial nations' constitutions. It's common to virtually all societies in today's global system excepting the few remaining pockets of indigenous and traditional peoples, who still assert the primacy of taking care of each other.

"Let freedom ring!" It's a powerful ideology to be sure. It's what constituted George W. Bush's second inauguration message and consequently is used to justify the military occupation of Iraq. But freedom is also what legitimates the Iraqi insurgent resistance against the U.S. invasion and occupation. Freedom is so embedded in our consciousness that it simultaneously inspires and inflames us. For those that don't have it, it means that they can't be all they can be and can't actualize their potential. Their fight for freedom is the struggle for more access, or equal access, to the means to be more tomorrow than they are today. Their "problem" with freedom—their lack of it—is that other people can self-actualize in a way that they can't.

Freedom is Insatiable Because Being More is Insatiable

Insatiable freedom goes hand in hand with the cultural imperative of being all you can be. The cultural imperative is not the result of capitalism but the cause of it. Capitalism is a symptom, or effect, of our unique culture. Freedom is meaningless if there is nothing else that humans could be other than what they are. Animals, on the other hand, don't have this freedom. They can't set about being more tomorrow than they are today. The freedom that we are talking about is the freedom to change how we are, to be other than what we are at a particular moment, to actualize or realize our potential. You can't be more if you don't have this freedom. It is an existential fact of being human.

But the focus of our existential freedom is our Selves—that we can end-lessly develop and improve ourselves and all that is good in the human world. Our culture says, "You *should* be more; you *should* strive to actualize your potential. But don't forget that your potential is infinite and insatiable." It's not something that you should do for awhile and then quit, because it is the defining feature of your life. "You are what you become," it says. In fact, our freedom culture says, "Life is about always becoming more and never should be limited to simply 'being.'"

No wonder people say that capitalism is the best of all possible worlds. If the purpose of life as a human is to insatiably self-actualize, improve, and develop, then capitalism is the perfect mechanism to assure that people stay on track. The system says, "You *must* be more tomorrow, because if you aren't, you may get left behind in the competitive struggle, or you will be a loser and not effectively earn your security." Capitalism is the whip that enforces the moral and social imperative of our culture. It compels us to pursue self-development for fear of economic hardship or moral condemnation by our peers. But it's not really the root of the problem. It's merely the best type of economy humans have come up with in order to further their real goal: insatiable development and improvement. It has all of the social triggers to motivate us toward actualization and continuous improvement. If you have been successfully assimilated into this culture, then you'll want to seek out and pursue being more in economically productive ways. Even the concept of efficiency has been reprogrammed to emphasize productivist values. Jeremy Rifkin states that, "efficiency became the indispensable tool for assuring personal success and the realization of the American Dream. He who is the most efficient, and therefore most productive, goes the reasoning, is the most likely to rise to the top—to make something out of himself" (Rifkin 2004, 112). So find that career niche that allows you to channel your being-more ability into having more, as well.

The cultural imperative of being more has become an enormous weight—an anchor tethered to our being. We measure people by their accomplishments and achievements. We make a virtue out of "striving," and "being driven," regardless of whether or not such behavior leads to more accomplishments. Rifkin adds that "for us, happiness is bound up in personal accomplishments, not the least being our individual material successes" (Rifkin 2004, 118). And would any of us have guilt about not being more if it was merely the economy that drove us to it? If you're not on the be all you can be treadmill, you subject yourself to either being a loser—wasting your potential—or feeling guilty about rejecting the competitive struggle of meeting others' expectations.

Here's a typical example mentioned to me recently by a friend working in "student development" at a college in the Midwest. He says

> Something else that might interest you....I had to do a 'development' session today with some student affairs people. I used the quote from your book [*Insatiable Is Not Sustainable*], 'By always wanting to be more, we are implicitly expressing our discontent with who we are. This makes us today creatures of permanent discontent.' Anyway, I thought you should know that everyone in the room not only disagreed with the quote, but wanted to explain to me that if we weren't improving we wouldn't be growing and that it is important to grow as professionals.

Our culture of insatiable freedom is the foundation for American capitalism and the American Dream. Citing Benjamin Franklin, Rifkin concludes that Franklin "believed that happiness was obtained by ceaseless personal improvement—that is, making something out of oneself" (Rifkin 2004, 25). And Hertsgaard adds that "our dominant religion, Protestantism, has preached a work ethic that instills guilt in anyone not striving to get ahead" (Hertsgaard 2002, 118-9). In fact, the productivist culture is stronger here than anywhere. America, says Rifkin, "is a land dedicated to possibilities, a place where constant improvement is the only meaningful compass and progress is regarded to be as certain as the rising sun" (Rifkin 2004, 16). The point is that we have even hinged our notion of happiness to be all you can be. Self-development, like the popular ideas of "continuous improvement" and "life-long learning," is a dynamic process in which humans are constantly "becoming" rather than content with their "being."

Invidious Self-Development

The economist/sociologist, Thorstein Veblen, not only coined the term, conspicuous consumption, but understood over a century ago that there's more to capitalism than meeting material needs. He made good use out of another term: invidiousness (Veblen [1899] 1945). It refers to the behavior of arousing envy in others. Veblen was mostly concerned with the extent in capitalism for people to use the system of production and consumption for purposes of status and what he called, "invidious distinction." We would say that its fundamental function is to meet material needs, and Veblen agreed, but with a caveat: capitalism is also a way to impress other people, pump up your self-esteem, and play the game of "I'm better than you." Such is particularly true with the have all you can have sphere of consumerism—the more I own, accumulate, and conspicuously consume goods, the more successful I am. Of course, it is not enough to simply *be* financially successful; you also have to show it off to other folks around you—that is, be conspicuous about it. Make them envy you. It raises your status and social esteem. You then demonstrate "pecuniary prowess."

The "keeping up with the Joneses" notion is not new to us. Veblen is remarkable because he figured this out over a hundred years ago and before the age of affluenza and overconsumption had matured. Today, Veblen's theory that capitalism is as much about proving one's status as it is about meeting needs, has deepened and widened with the fuller assimilation of be all you can be. It is more stressful than ever. Why? Because, rather than demonstrating success by *having* more than others, we feel the need to demonstrate it by *being* more.

There are a growing number of people who have increasingly rejected the have all you can have barometer of social esteem. But they haven't rejected the productivist criterion of be all you can be. That's what we mean by invidious self-development. Your family may react with some alarm when you mention that you aren't into money, a big house, a new SUV, or any of the smorgasbord of luxury toys flooding the market. But if you respond and say that your passion is music, surfing, or any other activity that taps your potentiality, they will settle down. As long as you can convince them that you are trying to be all you can be and insatiably self-develop in one of these ways, they will be dutifully impressed. Your social esteem will be restored. Why? Because we as a culture measure each other on the basis of our socially acceptable accomplishments—whatever they may be. You are condemned to be judged by your achievements—your self-development—whether it pays well or not.

In Figure 2.2 it's both performism and consumerism that can demonstrate self-development prowess. During Veblen's time, people mostly focused on the way in which consumption and wealth demonstrated status. Now, that's been extended to include performance of any kind. In fact, one might argue that it has always been about demonstrating self-development. Only in earlier periods, it was consumption of goods that was the socially legitimized way to measure it. Today, it's not only money that we use, but all kinds of self-improving and actualizing activities. There are more opportunities for this than ever before—another marvel of capitalism.

Consequently, what Veblen did was reveal a feature of capitalism that adds to our stressful living: it's a game; it has no end. If the system was only about meeting material needs, it might conceivably have a limit. Even though a principle tenet of economics is that people's wants are insatiable, one might argue that at some point they become pretty well satiated with stuff and turn to other pursuits. But if, as Veblen implies, the system is also a vehicle for people's efforts to obtain esteem and status, there's no logical limit. The quest for esteem and status is competitive for one thing and is played like a game with no end. As soon as one person demonstrates a degree of self-development and others follow suit, then another raises the bar. It goes on and on, like chasing a phantom goal that's always out of reach.

And it's not limited to individuals but includes organizations, as well. Both between and within organizations there is a relatively new phenomenon occurring. Rather than the relevant authority, whether bosses, corporate HQ, or the national office, dictating the height of the productivist hoop that people are supposed to jump through, the new twist is to allow them the "freedom" to set their own goals. It's a catch-22 in some respects, because if the goal is set pretty low, it is easy to jump through and minimizes the stress. You've demonstrated your ability to accomplish things. The problem is that the superiors are wise to this—you're still a slacker. On the other hand, you can set your goals extremely high, above your peers and colleagues. This looks good, but you may not clear the bar. Admirable goals but failure to measure up. So what do you do? Try to set your goals as high as possible, such that you have to strain to clear the bar, but still succeed. Don't set it too low, and don't set it too high, but just high enough to demonstrate your successful productivism. There's stress with this, because you have to grope your own way through it. It's not "How high can you jump?" But "How high can you set your bar and still make it?" It's a remarkably workable technique for career labor, as it demonstrates a host of productivist values from self-discipline to tenacity, determination, ambition, and accomplishment.

The ratcheting effect exists as a result of the fact that human potential is always out of reach. As far as we know, there's no logical limit to our ability to always be more tomorrow than we are today. But when people buy into the cultural imperative to insatiably self-actualize and there's an esteem issue linked to it, then there's no end to either the stress or the guilt. It's pretty easy to buy into the esteem game, because, as we have argued, we're all insecure—capitalism's trump card to get us motivated. "You're on your own, pal."

Today's Hypercapitalism

About twenty years ago *Business Week* opened with a three-page ad by GTE that announced, "Business Is War" (Bluestone and Harrison 1988, 21). They were right, of course, and if anything has changed it is that the war has intensi-fied. This is all part of the globalization of capitalism that has advanced by leaps with the continuing progression of the high tech revolution in communications and computerization. It's a phenomenon to which most of us have become all too familiar, since it has been accompanied by outsourcing of several million jobs in the past decade; downsizing and streamlining of domestic production; increased job insecurity and competition; more part-time labor; the "jobless re-covery" after the 2001 recession; and the record foreign trade and balance of payments deficits.

Besides the internationalization of production and its compete-or-die busi-ness climate, the high tech revolution has meant speed—hypercapitalism, in Jeremy Rifkin's words. "The onslaught of new technology, which promised to set us free, has instead ratcheted up the rhythms of everyday life," according to Jay Walljasper (2003, 62). He adds that "in our industrialized, fast-paced soci-ety, we too often view time as just another mechanical instrument to be pro-grammed." And with so little alone-time, "every spare moment becomes an op-portunity to make another connection" (Rifkin 2000, 208). The connections he's talking about are people. What you know in the "age of access" is still vitally important, but who you know and how you network and market yourself are more relevant than ever.

Even though hypercapitalism is an accelerated version of its post-World War II predecessor, it has also created social heterogeneity and simultaneously economic homogeneity. Paradoxically, we witness dis-integration of many tradi-tional ethnic and social enclaves that have previously escaped the dislocating effects of marketization and capitalism, but there is social re-integration in all manner of novel ways. With human and capital mobility at dizzying rates, a city like Los Angeles becomes a microcosm of a new multi-cultural, multi-lingual pastiche—a collage of contradictory cultural features where nothing "fits" because the norm is "everything fits" (Kunstler 1998; Soja 1989). It's the postmodern eclectic lifestyle (Harvey 1989; Jameson 1991; Lash and Urry 1987; Rifkin 1991). Continuity is out; fragmentation is in. But the heterogeneity is mostly social. With the economic sphere, it is quite the opposite: Americanization; McWorld; Everytown, USA; Sprawlmart; BigBox-Franchise-FastFood Corporatism.

So, on the one hand, when you glance down a commercial Main Street in Anytown, the physical appearance is not a caricature of a standardized, homogenized, and sanitized McStreet—it's the real thing. But what is different is the composition of its consumers. They are increasingly diverse in ethnicity, religion, race, gender, and lifestyle. With the proliferation of lifestyle subcultures, we are equally likely to see a Muslim female talking on a cell phone in Spanish, as we are a male teenager, dressed like a skater and listening to Afro-pop on a headset. It's not simply diversity between ethnicities and cultures, but within them, as well. What they have in common is not language or culture, but shopping. They're all entering or exiting the Golden Arches. While surely the basest, a Big Mac may be the only common denominator. Hungarian social theorists Agnes Heller and Ferenc Feher stated in the late 1980s that

> The specter of 'mass society' in which everyone likes the same, needs the same, practices the same, was a short intermezzo in Europe and North America. What has indeed emerged is not the standardization and unification of consumption, but rather the enormous pluralization of tastes, practices, enjoyments and needs (1988, 142).

The freedom apparent in these images is real enough, and although this is further evidence of the culture of insatiable freedom, it also suggests a new stress experience: mass identity crisis. Almost four decades ago (1967), French social theorist, Michel Foucault, an icon of postmodern philosophy, stated

> We are in the epoch of simultaneity: we are in the epoch of juxtaposition, the epoch of the near and far, of the side-by-side, of the dispersed. We are at a moment, I believe, when our experience of the world is less that of a long life developing through time than that of a network that connects points and intersects with its own skein (1986, 22).

His reference to networks is prophetic since that has become one the defining features of today's "age of access" (Rifkin 2000). Rifkin adds that "in the 19th century, one's sense of self was far more static. It wasn't uncommon to think of one's life as a product whose value increases over time. In the 20th century, people slowly came to think of themselves more as works in process. 'Being' gave way to 'becoming' in the new streamlined world" (202). The Self is now in a state of perpetual change and flux.

This creates what Fredric Jameson calls "psychic fragmentation," stating that in our globalized, here-today-gone-tomorrow culture the isolated individual has been decentered (Jameson 1991). What we do and experience faces the "challenge of accelerating turnover time and the rapid write-off of traditional and historically acquired values" (Harvey 1989, 291). The decentered Self exists today in a whirling dust devil of relationships. Who am I? How do I ground myself? Do I have any social or cultural foundation to steady me? Is competition all that matters? These become the pressing questions we ask ourselves.

The severity of psychological insecurity has intensified with hypercapitalism right along with that of material insecurity. Is it a case of "adapt, get connected, or die?" Rifkin suggests that the youth of the industrial world are quickly adapting. They are becoming the "new archetype human," as "customs, conventions, and traditions are virtually nonexistent in their fast-paced, ever changing environment" (Rifkin 2000, 187). It's a case of "time-space compression" (Harvey 1989), and we are increasingly losing any sense of bearing. What's left is one's unease that only transcendence matters—focus your being on becoming. Either go with the flow or go your own way but keep on trying to be more. Suffer the stress, rather than the guilt; just don't get too exhausted.

Part Three

The System is a Victim of Your Ancestors

Our Leaver and Taker Ancestry

To argue that we are victims of the system and then maintain that the system itself is a victim of our ancestors implies an historic and evolutionary approach to today's problems. Our culture of insatiable freedom and our insatiable improver economy are themselves an effect of what's preceded us, in other words. We shouldn't blame capitalism for all of the stress we experience. The question is, "Where did capitalism and its freedom culture come from?"

Although we can't and don't want to go back, we need to look back. There are two watersheds that stand out, and Daniel Quinn's interpretation of the first is at the cutting edge of today's crisis over sustainability. Karl Polanyi's analysis of the second is less profound but unrivaled. The first watershed in human history is the Agricultural Revolution—the Neolithic Revolution. This began about 10,000 years ago. It marks the emergence of the earliest civilizations. The second is the genesis of capitalist civilization in the 16th century—a strangely unique appearance.

Quinn's thesis is that all human societies prior to the Neolithic Revolution were "leaver" societies (Quinn 1992, 1996, 1997, 1999). They were tribal, small, personal, hunting and gathering clans. Whether they were *Homo erectus* or *Homo sapiens* they were leavers in the sense that they left control over the world to the gods—more specifically, they organized life with the understanding that *they belonged to the earth*. This was true for the better part of a million-and-a-half years of trekking the planet. But with civilization and its inhabitants things changed dramatically. The Neolithic Revolution occurred after the last

Ice Age about 10,000–15,000 years ago. It was a slow development, and an evolutionary process but still conspicuously different than hunting and gathering. At that time there were about five to ten million humans.

Homo sapiens, our direct forebears, began their migration out of Africa 100,000 years ago and eventually displaced the one other species that had populated much of Europe and Asia—*Homo erectus*. They were both leavers. *Homo sapiens* left Africa in part due to food scarcity in northern regions of the continent, and it has been estimated that their numbers might have decreased to as few as 10,000 when they undertook their trek.

What happened to *Homo erectus* is still debated. Having left Africa over a million-and-a-half years ago, they had adapted, at least in Western and Central Europe, to very cold and harsh living conditions. Their physical features (their noses—huge by today's standards—were able to warm the cold air they inhaled) actually evolved over 250,000 years to make their lives sustainable. They were short, squatty, had elemental language, ate predominately meat, but reproduced their ways in a sustainable fashion. They had fire, flint blades, clothing, and spears for stabbing rather than throwing. They ate about 4,000 calories per day, and evolved teeth and stomachs specifically for chewing and digesting their meat diet. Many were, of course, cave dwellers, who were able to avoid overuse of their immediate surroundings. Neanderthals evolved the most successful human economy ever experienced, if we measure success by the longevity of their species. They are the only species to actually have evolved physical characteristics specific to cold climate conditions.

The Cro-Magnons, *Homo sapiens*, began their migration out of Africa by walking across the Red Sea at its southern tip, where it meets the Gulf of Aden. There may have been as few as 250 of them wading across a ten mile stretch called the "Gates of Grief," as it is known today. Once in Yemen they then walked across the Strait of Hormuz at the Persian Gulf. They continued along the coast of the Indian Ocean as sustainable and successful beach combers. Eventually they built rafts and floated from the southern tip of Indonesia to the Australian continent—a destination reached about 70,000 years ago. Others migrated northward into Asia, Europe, and eventually some walked across the Bering Strait to North America. Evidence suggests that this might have happened about 20,000–25,000 years BP. They migrated to South America first, while the first human presence discovered in North America is at the Meadowcroft site in Ohio—about 15,000 years BP. In Germany 20,000–30,000 years ago they encountered their "sibling species"—the Neanderthals. The paleoanthropic debate concerns the extent to which they either assimilated or extincted the Neanderthals. *Homo sapiens* was a taller, warm-adapted people, with more advanced, thus more communicative language skills, spears that they threw, and more tailored clothing for agility and dexterity.

Yet as leaver peoples both species were content to leave nature to its own devices, its own rhythms, and its own course. They evolved a form of satiable living, taking care of each other, using collective and cooperative labor, living simply and harmoniously within the community of life as they found it. There is no evidence that they were motivated by self-interest or the desire to improve. As Quinn says, they competed with other tribes but didn't wage war. They practiced the Erratic Retaliator strategy when competing between tribes and clans— "give as good as you get, but don't be too predictable." This is quite at odds with what happened later with civilization—the Annihilator strategy (Quinn 1997, 90-91). In fact, even though aggression appears to be a universal trait beginning with our earliest ancestors, "organized group conflict is first attested only about 10,000 years ago" (Wyse and Winkleman [1988] 1997, 44). The evidence for this is from a site near the Egyptian-Sudanese border where a prehistoric cemetery contained about 58 bodies in which half appear to have experienced death by violence—stone blades were found embedded in the bones of some skeletons (44). Archeological evidence suggests that it was with the growth of agriculture that group conflict became violent.

But leavers were excellent problem-solvers, developed a type of security-through-community, were focused on sufficiency rather than efficiency, and were surely minimalists. They were not economic maximizers, trying to minimize effort or get the most for the least. As nomads they couldn't afford to be hoarders or possession accumulators. They frequently threw their tools away, only to make more when and if needed. They didn't economize as we do today. All our anthropological findings suggest one thing—Daniel Quinn's insight: they didn't seek to control, dominate, engineer, govern, shape, influence, or bend nature to their will. They lived with it rather than over it. And this worked for them.

But with the emergence of civilization, what were leaver peoples—our Paleolithic ancestors—became takers (Quinn 1992). Through the lengthy process of settling down, farming, domesticating animals, and building up permanent towns and cities, the taker way emerged. What does it mean? What were these civilized people taking and no longer leaving? It's not land, resources, or food, but more importantly, control. Fundamentally, leavers becoming takers means getting control over nature, the community of life, and other people, as well. Takers, in effect, are about taking control over the natural world, and usurping what leavers had left to the gods—control. For takers, *the earth belongs to us*.

Why the need for control as people turned from hunting and gathering to agriculture? Although it's not exclusively an issue of settled farming, once this began to happen, for example, in the Tigris and Euphrates river valleys around 11,000 years BP, cities like Jericho could thrive. It is the oldest known settled farming community. The essential discovery, without which there would have been no Jericho, was that seeds could be planted in one place—they are what make barley and wheat plants grow. And water can be transferred by irrigation techniques to drier land. Jericho, in particular, is a result of the discovery of bread wheat. Bread wheat was different than many of the other grains, because it had a larger kernel and didn't blow off the stalk of the plant as easily as some (Wyse and Winkleman [1988] 1997, 80).

What's the bottom line? Expansion. What the Agricultural Revolution did was give people a knowledge and recognition of expansion of all kinds. Population can expand indefinitely with what Quinn calls "totalitarian agriculture." Of course, there's a price. Quinn states that "totalitarian agriculture is more than a means of getting what you need to live, it's the foundation for the most laborious lifestyle ever developed on this planet" (Quinn 1996, 248-9). What he's suggesting is a finding by archeologists that although settled farming was a way to solve a problem stemming from population growth and accompanying food scarcity, it was also much more time-consuming and involved greater inputs of labor. It took more work that hunting and gathering, but could produce far more food, as well.

With more people, the settled takers can grow more food, build more housing, produce more tools, and increase their goat herds. Civilization gave people a new sense for controlling their fate. They could expand and grow, improve, and develop as a result of one thing: control over the community of life, the natural world, and other humans. Civilization brought innovations in language, writing, art, music, and all that we are familiar with when the topic turns to its marvels and how we should be thankful that it happened.

But civilizations also brought economic and social classes and hierarchical decision making. It created pyramids of both stone and authority. With the economic surpluses growth created, some could live off the labor of others. Those at the top could exercise control over those at the bottom and bend them to their will. It is with takerism and the Agricultural Revolution that group conflict becomes violent. The desire to control begets both inequality and violent aggression. Slave and feudal societies evolved based fundamentally on making the subordinate classes economically dependent on the rulers. Finding a way to deprive the ruled access to land and food has always been the key to this. And, as we know, it continues to be the case today.

To be sure, civilizations have always been patriarchal and classist. It's men who have always been at the top, regardless of where we look. They have ruled women and other men. The control has brought expansion and more products, technology, improvements, and stuff in general, but it's also meant more work— at least for the people at the bottom. The taker way meant domination of people and nature, above all.

Yet we must not forget that the taker way of control, expansion, and domination only reflected a minority of humankind when it started. Until very recently, most people continued to live as leavers—who are increasingly fighting to maintain their access to land and resources to avoid the leash of economic dependency. What are left of them today are the native and indigenous remnants of our past. Unlike the Neanderthals' encounter with *Homo sapiens*, the takers have not completely extincted or assimilated the leavers. Not yet.

Figure 3.1 indicates the human time line with respect to leavers and takers.

Figure 3.1. A Short History of Humankind I:
"Takers Swamp Leavers"

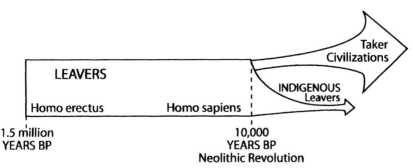

The point is that the taker way, that is, civilization, is powerful enough that it doesn't have to respect leavers. Leavers tend to get in the way of civilization. Although leavers walked 100,000 miles around the earth in 100,000 years—surely an accomplishment by today's standards, they did this with little population growth. The migration out of Africa continued after our first ancestors left by crossing the Gates of Grief. In the 100,000 years that *Homo sapiens* trekked about, population growth was about two-thousandths of a percent per year. It took almost 30,000 years to double it.

With taker civilizations emerging 10,000 years ago population growth rates accelerated dramatically. Quinn states that "growth at an infinitesimal rate became growth at a rapid rate. Starting at ten million, our population doubled not in nineteen thousand years but in five thousand years, bringing it to twenty million. The next doubling—doubling and a bit—took only two thousand years, bringing us to fifty million" (Quinn 1996, 288). Of course the reason that takers could grow increasingly rapidly is, as Quinn says: they realized they could circumvent the food scarcity constraint that had previously kept leaver populations in balance with food supply. With settled civilizations if population began to increase, then takers could bring more land into cultivation and feed more people. More people didn't create food scarcity as it did with hunters and gatherers and the rest of the community of life. The balancing process of nature, as we know, is that more population puts pressure on available food supply. With food becoming scarce, population growth slows down. Consequently, food becomes more plentiful triggering a new round of population growth. Such was the case for millions of years.

With takers, more people simply meant more growth in the "means of life"—food, shelter, clothing, and other necessities. Easy enough for sedentary people who then also figured out novel technologies to push the process ever onward. Today we are reluctant to recognize limits to this. More economic growth, more population growth; more population growth, more economic growth. More stuff, more people; more people, more stuff. Remarkably in the last half-century, the world's population has more than doubled, bringing us beyond six billion. The stuff, global output, has quadrupled. For today's remaining leavers, it's a different story, of course. Either they haven't wanted to, haven't had to, or haven't needed to buy into the takers' self-reproducing system of perpetual expansion. But there aren't many of them left. They've been swamped by the "taker thunderbolt" as Quinn says.

Taker Thunderbolt Becomes Capitalist Juggernaut

Although the handful of taker civilizations that have preceded today's market system were often dynamic with great stability and therefore longevity, they pale in comparison to capitalist civilization. When Polanyi examined the "great transformation," he was thinking exclusively of the 16th–19th centuries in Western Europe. The drama was being played out there between the feudal/medieval system, known for its constraints on personal freedom, and the novel but suspect infant of capitalism/political democracy. But the great transformation has continued inexorably to expand and enclose over ninety percent of the planet. Not only leavers but all other types of civilizations can't measure up to capitalism. The ideologues of capitalism when they say that it is the "best of all possible worlds" are emphasizing this point. Figure 3.2 illustrates it. Of the variety of taker civilizations, the most common—slavery and feudalism—have been dead-ended.

Figure 3.2. A Short History of Humankind II:
"Capitalism Swamps Everything"

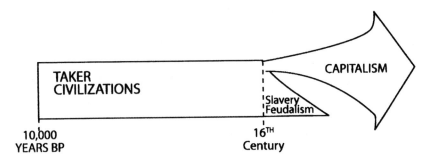

Unlike the earliest civilizations, where several started simultaneously in different locations, capitalism started only in Europe, and it required colonial plundering and the pillaging of native peoples over most of the world to make a go of it. Estimates of the flow of wealth into Europe in the 16th century suggest that it experienced a three-fold net increase in total wealth resulting from the slave trade and gold and silver inflows. This has been well documented (Wolfe 1997; Wallerstein 1974, 1980; Ponting 1991; Cameron 1989). So the juggernaut of capitalist growth got revved up quickly with the help of the slave trade, gold pillaging in Africa and South America, and the enclosure of the "commons"— eviction of peasants and serfs from common lands worldwide. And today, with the dismantling of the former Soviet Union, most proudly applaud it as a triumph of a system—*the* system—driven by our sacred principle of freedom.

Karl Polanyi didn't dispute any of this. He simply called our attention to its uniqueness. A market economy, he stated in 1944,

> implies a self-regulating system of markets ... an economy directed by market prices and nothing but market prices. Such a system capable of organizing the whole of economic life without outside help or interference would certainly deserve to be called self-regulating. These rough indications should suffice to show the entirely unprecedented nature of such a venture in the history of the race. No society could, naturally, live for any length of time unless it possessed an economy of some sort; but previously to our time no economy has ever existed that, even in principle, was controlled by markets. Though the institution of the market was fairly common since the later Stone Age, its role was no more than incidental to economic life ([1944] 1957, 43).

The idea that humans could actually create a "system" that would simultaneously allow the exercise of unbridled self-interest and meet the material needs of the majority was largely unthinkable until four hundred years ago. And capitalism was met with plenty of skepticism.

Most of its early critics were moral philosophers, and by 1850 this included Karl Marx. They suspected that any system based on pursuit of economic self-interest and driven by personal greed would result in social anarchy and chaos. The thought of everyone in society let loose to do whatever they wanted, where and when they wanted, was abhorrent. Yet it was Adam Smith in Glascow, Scotland in 1776, himself a moral philosopher, who drafted the first logical and comprehensive defense of such a system (*The Wealth of Nations*). It was market competition—the invisible hand, he believed, that would reconcile self-interest with general interest. The system was dynamic and resilient enough to weather the storm of the Industrial Revolution. By 1900, most workers in Europe had made substantial gains, gotten the vote, and thought they had more to lose than their chains.

Polanyi didn't try to make the case that capitalism, a "free" market economy, wouldn't work. His point was that such a system was rather unstable if left totally to its own devices. It might have depressions, unemployment, poverty wages, sweatshop working conditions, and serious inequality and discrimination. The neoclassical economists today argue precisely the opposite—the more intense the competition and insecurity of all competitors, the more stable the system. It's all about the notion of equilibrium: static, dynamic, micro, macro, and general equilibrium. Homoeostasis, like something that might occur in natural systems.

But the free market economy has never been all that free. Historically, as Polanyi documented, as soon as capitalism became disembedded, when people were freed from feudal constraints, and markets took over, they immediately sought protection from the insecurities of market-driven competition. The mixed economy, Social Democracy, and the welfare state have been the result. Government, unions, trusts, conglomerates, patents, and collusive oligopolies have cushioned businesses and workers. Polanyi calls this the "protective response."

Earlier taker civilizations did not motivate their subjects by the insecurity of "you're on your own, pal." Obligation and command were the most common incentives. It wasn't a case of sink-or-swim, but of "doing what you're told" to do by lords, masters, and religious authorities. Absent was today's focus on individual freedom, but predecessor civilizations placed requirements on their dominant classes to see to it that the mass of unfree subjects were taken care of—rather like the security of a prison. The elites weren't obligated to free the slaves or serfs, nor were they obligated to give away their wealth, privilege, or power. It was simply a cultural norm to care for them in a paternalistic fashion.

Putting Daniel Quinn's contribution together with Karl Polanyi's gives us a uniquely comprehensive view of our past. With the Agricultural Revolution Quinn calls our attention to the split between leavers and takers, then with capitalism's emergence in the 16th century, Polanyi reveals the split between security and freedom. In effect there are two dichotomies shaping our modernist, increasingly stressful lives: takers versus leavers and security versus freedom. As takers we are all about control and expansion, domination of nature and the life process itself. Then as insecure takers *we are driven*—compelled and coerced—to control, expand, dominate, insatiably actualize, develop, and improve, whether it does us in or not. In the developed world, particularly in the United States, we have (unequal) freedom and lots of stuff. The remainder of the world, which doesn't have either, desperately desires both. Finally, there are the leaver enclaves who can't relate to any of it. It hasn't always been this way for humanity. We've become the *driven takers*. But don't misunderstand this. You may be neither driven nor a taker. These terms are not intended to be taken personally. It's the society in which we live, the system and the culture that are driven and takers. It's not about any of us in particular but all of us in general. It's our condition, circumstances, and situation.

Driven Takers: An Aberration of an Aberration

We can modify the two previous diagrams (Figure 3.1 and 3.2) to look like Figure 3.3. It has one message drawn from Daniel Quinn and Karl Polanyi: civilization is an aberration, and capitalism is an aberration of civilization itself.

Figure 3.3. The Aberration of an Aberration

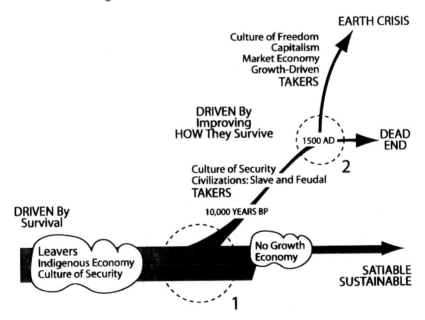

First, we need to be clear about what is meant by the term, aberration. To call both civilization and capitalist civilization aberrations doesn't mean that they aren't successful, are bad, or failed systems. What it does suggest is that the evolutionary continuum of the community of life is the one indicated by leaver peoples along the base line of the diagram. The base line leading towards today's remaining leavers is an evolutionary path emphasizing satiability and assured security. These are the two pivotal features that will perhaps save you and the world—*if* humanity undertakes the necessary cultural revolution of sustainability.

But at Point One, a freak event happened: takerism struck out on its own. Then again at Point Two, another weird event occurred: the market society split from the civilization path and dead-ended its predecessors. Our experience with post-One living is less than one percent of our history, while our post-Two experience is only five percent of our taker history, and a miniscule fraction of all of it. But conventional wisdom reverses this. It says that nothing about being human actually counted for much before Point One, while today, we are told, what is the tiniest bit of our experience, capitalism/modernism since Point Two, counts for everything (Quinn 1992, 1996). Figure 3.4 shows it as we've been led to believe.

Figure 3.4. A Taker View of History

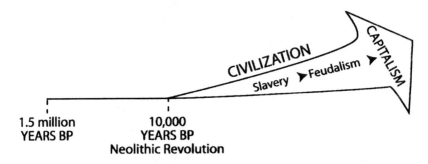

Not much happens until the Neolithic Revolution; since then it's been the upward march of civilizational improvement culminating with our current global capitalism. The ideologues tell us that all that's left for the future of humankind is more of the upward march of growth, more and better living, for more and better people—and capitalism is the end of civilization's evolution—the best of all possible worlds.

Had the emergence of civilizations been widespread and universal, we wouldn't refer to it as an aberration. But the Upper Paleolithic period (35,000–12,000 years BP) was unusual in part because the last Ice Age ended during it, and with major climatic fluctuations, along with retreating ice sheets, hunters and gatherers witnessed greater food abundance, more rain, and available water. There were technological changes, as well. Blades replaced flakes and created more precision cutting tools, spears, fish nets, and hooks (blades were produced by the new pressure flaking technique which meant that they could be sharper and longer than their precursor, the stone flaking tool). Hunting continued to be the basis for the Upper Paleolithic economy, however (Wyse and Winkleman [1988] 1997, 72-73).

The result of this was population growth and ultimately pressure on food supply. The discoveries of herding wild animals, initially goats, and planting seeds did not happen overnight. Animal domestication and growing crops were thousands of years in the making. But eventually, by 10,000 years ago, farming was found to be a solution to the population-food scarcity problem. It's important to view this revolution for what it is: problem-solving knowledge.

As environmental historian, Clive Ponting says, "human societies did not set out to invent 'agriculture' and permanent settlements. Rather a series of marginal changes were made gradually in existing ways of obtaining food as a result of particular local circumstances" (Ponting 1991, 38). Ponting argues that there is a long continuum of incremental changes from hunting and gathering to settled farming, much of which was based on the exchange of tools and knowledge between groups. "In certain restricted regions of the Old World—," say Wyse and Winkleman, "the Fertile Crescent of the Near East, the hill country of Pakistan, the plains of northern China, and the Yangtze delta—hunter-gatherer communities began to experiment with locally available plants and animals in a way which ultimately led to their domestication" (Wyse and Winkleman [1988] 1997, 76).

One conclusion is clear: this was not a case of "an idea whose time had come." Where hunting and gathering faced no food scarcity, where populations didn't put pressure on the land, farming was not undertaken. In regions like Japan, northwestern Europe, and sub-Saharan Africa there was abundant enough food to support population growth without turning to agriculture. But population globally continued to grow such that by 6,000 years ago farming was common over most of the Old World. On the other hand, most of the world's farmers were "leaver farmers." Not many of those who turned to farming were organized into civilizations and became takers.

Was the Agricultural Revolution bound to happen or is it an aberration? The paleontologists' evidence suggests it was an aberration. Experimentation, discovery, and some imagination were the driving features that allowed humans to solve a problem in a circumstance they didn't ask for.

There's another way in which this was an aberration. It created the notion of insatiability and "more"—more of life, more people, more actualization of potential, more development and improvement. As hunters and gatherers, leaver peoples were largely nomadic, of course. Even though more than one generation might forage and hunt in the same thirty mile radius, they moved frequently enough as the seasons changed, that they were less likely to observe how food and animals can multiply from one year to the next. Additionally, as early as 1.8 million years ago, with *Homo erectus* at the Olduvai Gorge site in Tanzania, there is evidence of shelters, which suggests that the inhabitants had home bases to which they brought back food (Wyse and Winkleman [1988] 1997). Still, it was a gathering lifestyle—it requires people to be in continual movement over their landscape.

Once our ancestors became sedentary, their ability to observe how growth takes place was greatly improved. Clearly, when nomads are on the move with the changing seasons, it is hard to visually notice "more" plants than in previous seasons. And it is more difficult to observe animal herds actually increasing in size. They surely realized that climate and weather were critical factors in determining the relative abundance of grains and herds. But once they became farmers, their ability to actually control growth would have been obvious to them. It's about "control" over nature, the defining feature of being takers and the extent to which (by staying in one place), they could easily observe how control creates "more"—more animals, more food, more development and improvement.

So the aberration of civilization is this: it demonstrated to humans that control yields more. Control exercised by farming, although labor intensive in a way they hadn't experienced, brought huge increases in productivity. With this, they had enough economic surplus over basic necessities to not only feed more people, but build pyramids, support permanent privileged classes, develop language and the arts.

As hunters and gatherers, humans were part of an ever-changing landscape in which everything alive was in seasonal motion. Hunters and gatherers were an embedded feature of that motion, so it would have been difficult for them to witness the effects of asserting control. It took settling down for people to fully understand how control can create more of all that humans might relish. It required the sedentary lifestyle to give humans the idea that not only could they create more from the natural world, but they as people could have and be more. And another important message was not only that more effective control could lead to more development, but that this had no inherent limits. It was insatiable. Therefore, the logical conclusion drawn from the Agricultural Revolution was that even if nature wasn't insatiable, it could be made that way. And this awareness no doubt followed from the awareness that humans had the capacity to use their control to insatiably actualize their own potential. The notion that humans exist as the potential to always become more—that it's an existential feature of our being—also emerges at this time. Control, more is better, insatiability, potentiality—these are the cultural legacies of the taker way.

With Point Two, the next evolutionary aberration, a new type of civilization began and has since swamped most of humankind—capitalism and its culture of freedom. It's an odd development, as well, because no other civilization had been based on the unlimited pursuit of individual self-interest. With the "great transformation," as Polanyi argued, economic behavior was no longer subordinated to social norms, customs, and traditions. Like the Agricultural Revolution, it too was accompanied by and through radical new technologies (the compass and telescope for navigation, three-crop rotation for increased food production, the printing press, and so on). The development of modern science and its application to industrial pursuits began in the watershed 16th century and fueled the subsequent cultural, political, and economic changes.

The aberration of capitalist civilization was based upon the universalization of be all you can be. And it was coerced by the fact of insecurity—"you're on your own, pal." For the first time in human history people were motivated to produce by virtue of individual insecurity, and that meant greater incentive to try to be more—to actualize and realize their potential. Between the Agricultural Revolution and the 16th century when the next aberration occurred, humans had evolved the ideas of being and having more, but these were not the driving forces that they became with capitalism. In fact, the concept of the individual is quite new and particularly the notion that all individuals can be and have more. Clearly, in the civilizations that preceded capitalism, there were elite classes who knew and understood human potentiality and the idea of social and personal growth and expansion. We see this in the fine arts and performing arts that were integral expressions of their achievements.

But for the most part, the principle or norm of be all you can be or have all you can have was reserved for the elites and privileged classes, frequently the clergy and those with recognized birth rights. Self-actualization of unlimited potential to be more was a restricted concept that simply didn't apply to commoners, slaves, serfs, or women. Most subjects of civilizations' male rulers were considered inferior by birth, intellect, ability, and aptitude. They were never to be like the gods or to aspire to such heights. More often they were expected to seek salvation rather than realize their potential. As we know, this was the ideological foundation for European feudalism after the fall of the Roman Empire. But it was common the world over. Even in Hellenic Greece during Aristotle and Plato's era (*c.* 350 BC), for all of their impressive and remarkable insights on democracy, freedom, and the individual, the Greek philosophers accepted slavery as a universal condition, relied on slaves to run and manage the farming estates, and viewed them as inferiors who needed to be cared for. Their view of women wasn't much different either.

What makes capitalist civilization so unique is that what had been an "idea" restricted to the few—be all you can be—became a universal motivator for the many. Along with forcing serfs and peasants off of the land and denying them access to resources of the commons, they were given freedom to move and seek opportunities wherever they could find them—"free" labor. At the same time that the subjugated classes (serfs who were tied to the land, yet unlike slaves who were tied to their masters) had their self-sufficient farm life taken away from them, the social and religious obligations of the Church and aristocracy to care for them were abandoned, as well. If you are totally on your own—a condition unknown in earlier systems—then your immediate salvation was to rely on your own initiative, talent, and skills. The end of the Christian Paternalist Ethic (Hunt 1990) meant the end of a cultural norm that had guided leavers and takers both for over a million years—the purpose of life is to take care of each other.

In other words, assured security was out and earned security was in. This could only have succeeded as a functional economic system if it included the essential incorporation of a new culture of freedom, inalienable rights of the individual, and democracy. It's no coincidence that the market system emerged simultaneously with representative and constitutional democracy. To motivate an economy on the basis of individual insecurity requires that players have a substantial realm of personal freedom in which to earn back their security.

For the interim period between the Agricultural Revolution and capitalism, the prevailing cultural norm was that of taking care of each other. While civilizations clearly had growth and development and sought improvements, these were not the driving forces or basic incentives. Their rulers were aware of how they, as special humans, could have and be more. They were aware of potential for self- and social-actualization. And they knew, most likely, that such capabilities were indeed insatiable. But they weren't driven by these ideas as we are today. The full assimilation of productivism and the social and moral imperative to always be more required the universalizing of individualism, democracy, and freedom in an economic system that required the removal of security.

A Short History of "Improvement"

We have been acculturated to a belief that humans have always sought improvements, regardless of whether or not they were leavers or takers, or regardless of whether or not they were hunters and gatherers before or after the Agricultural Revolution. People have always been insatiable improvers, we are told. The evidence that archeologists have uncovered about our Paleolithic ancestors suggests otherwise. Of course, today we are forced to make inferences, since they left no direct traces of what they thought about themselves, their being, and their motivations. But what they *did*, which paleontologists can piece together from artifacts, suggests that they *thought* much differently than we do today.

Our earliest direct ancestors are *Homo habilis*, whose skeletal remains found at Hadar, Ethiopia, date to 2.5 million years ago. This is the earliest discovery of tools. The tools are essentially pebbles with uneven but sharp edges that were created by using one stone as a hammer to chip away flakes from another (Wyse and Winkleman [1988] 1997, 56). Archeologists have also concluded that the flakes were used as tools, as well. Do we want to consider this as the first case of "insatiable improvement" driven by the genetic thirst to be all we can be? The Hadar site is the true beginning of archeology, but it's not evidence of insatiable improvers.

Our leaver ancestors were actually "satiable survivors." They were not driven by finding a better way, being more tomorrow, or growth. To the extent that we can say they were "driven," what we really mean is "motivated," and their goal was not to improve *how* they lived but to successfully survive. Then how do we account for the gradual and evolutionary accumulation of tools, technology, and improvements?

Improvements "happened." They were largely "accidental." These satiable survivors did not get up in the morning with a day planner that required one or more of them to devote the day to finding a better way to do this or that. Our archeological findings simply don't substantiate an improvement drive. The key words we encounter in the literature are words like, discover, recognize, imagine, problem solve, and create. They were smart enough to recognize and discover certain techniques that made a task easier, more convenient, less difficult, and so on. The fact that today we say they had improved their lives, or had improvements, doesn't suggest that they were actively seeking them as an expression of their being.

They shared information about techniques. "Early humans were probably highly social animals living in fairly permanent groups. The sharing of food, and the beginnings of a division of labor between males (concentrating on providing meat) and females (concentrating on providing plant foods), may have come about only gradually as hunting became more important" (Wyse and Winkleman [1988] 1997, 56). These improvements not only "happened" by discovery but they happened at a glacial pace. It took about one million years for hand axes, cleavers, and scrapers to evolve from the earliest Hadar tools. And it took another million years for wooden tools to be discovered.

Jacob Bronowski, whose classic, *The Ascent of Man* (1973), argues that the most consistent thread between us and them is in our common ability to imagine, be creative, recognize and discover what works, and have "flexibility of mind" to notice discoveries and make them "community property" (46). Bronowski states that our cultural evolution is "essentially a constant growing and widening of the human imagination" (56). He, as well as other paleontologists, does not say our common link is be all you can be. He adds that the slow reproduction of a way of living, a workable lifestyle, was based on the fact that "the only ambition of the son is to be like the father" (62). Repetition, in other words. But it was repetitive for a reason: it worked. Ponting asserts that it "was without doubt the most successful and flexible way of life adopted by humans and the one that caused the least damage to natural ecosystems" (Ponting 1991, 18).

As the driven takers or insatiable improvers that we have become today, it is hard to imagine being content to be like our parents in terms of technological improvements and progress in general. In fact, our parents don't want us to limit ourselves to being like them. They tell us to be productive and always be more and achieve more than they did. Leavers—satiable survivors—don't say this. Our ancestors and contemporary leavers figure that if it works, so be it. We moderns on the other hand say, "If it works, it can be made to work better."

Some additional support for our rethinking of ancient leaver peoples also comes from anthropological study of today's leavers. The economic anthropologist and former student of Karl Polanyi, Marshall Sahlins, stated in *Stone Age Economics* (1972) that early humans were not maximizers, not economizers, but were "uneconomic" instead. The first chapter is titled, "The Original Affluent Society," and he argues that leaver peoples, both then and now, have been able to obtain "affluence without abundance" due to a "kind of material plenty" (9). Largely because they had finite/limited needs, their ability to satisfy them came relatively easily, as well. Few needs—being satiable—easy to fulfill. Lots more free time, more leisure, no hurry, less stress. It amounts to the difference between the two *Mutts* cartoons you've seen. The first is our modern taker view and the second is the leaver view. Takers are insatiable, of course, and make a virtue out of it. Not leavers; not our ancestors.

There is also ample evidence that our leaver ancestors didn't care much about trying to get more, and in many regions worldwide, they had as many as four hours a day of down time. They had idle or excess productive capacity that went unused. They didn't care about trying to get the most for the least. They had "persistent under-exploitation of resources" (Sahlins 1972, 98). Their work days were relaxed and discontinuous—starting and stopping whenever they felt like it. In their workday there is evidence of "immoderate standards of relaxa- tion—or, what is probably a better understanding of the latter, very moderate standards of 'sufficient work'" (52). In fact, there was little separation between work and leisure. The Neanderthals were known to have spent several hours a day sitting idly, grooming each other's hair. This was part of their bonding be- havior. It signifies that life was about taking care of each other.

What we infer from our past and present leaver cultures are that these peo- ple were satiable, were not fixated on being more tomorrow, actualizing poten- tial, or developing their talents and achieving goals. They were minimalists who knew how to live lightly, justly, and simply with the earth and each other. Was it a struggle for existence, eking out a bare subsistence living? Times could be hard, but Sahlins and other anthropologists have argued persuasively that it was not a way of living that was as harsh as conventional wisdom maintains.

Was There Meaning and Purpose?

Clearly, the answer is yes. Their art suggests this. They had plenty of free time for making ornamentation, figurines, cave drawings, and so on. And if life had no meaning and purpose except for the struggle to survive, it's unlikely that there would have been any art at all. We are apt to think that if life was just a struggle to survive, then our ancestors must have consequently been driven-by-improvement to overcome it. But it doesn't fit. Life obviously made sense to them. Their art reflects self-worth and social-esteem, as well.

Another indicator of leavers' meaningful and purposeful living is deliberate burial of their dead. The earliest known cases date to the Neanderthals in Europe 120,000 years ago. Also, during the Middle Paleolithic period (80,000–35,000 years BP), there are widespread Neanderthal burial remains in much of Europe. And with *Homo sapiens* in the Upper Paleolithic period, burial was common and finds include a variety of ornaments buried with the individual. One such site near Moscow dating to 24,000 years BP contained a man buried with two dozen perforated fox teeth sewn on his cap and about 20 ivory bracelets. There were also two boys buried with a variety of pendants, ivory ornaments, and ivory spears. Amazingly, with each body there were 3,500 ivory beads arranged from head to toe. Estimates are that each bead would have required about 45 minutes of carving time, and therefore each of the three was buried with 2,625 hours worth of beadwork (Wise and Winkleman [1988] 1997, 34).

These finds suggest a lot about the meaning and purpose that leavers brought to their lives. They obviously cared for each other, cared about each other, took care of one another, had affection and emotions of joy and grief. They clearly had a measure of leisure and free time in which to reflect, create, and imagine. They apparently preferred to spend time in artistic pursuits rather than trying to improve their way of living. This evidence also implies that they cared more about taking care of each other than the individual ambition to achieve self-actualization. They must have practiced satiability, in other words.

Although ornamentation is common before the Upper Paleolithic period, it is with *Homo sapiens* during this era that both portable art—painting and carving of objects—and wall art became widespread in Europe. There have been hundreds of such finds dating to this period. They represent our ancestors' ability to think abstractly, to symbolize the meanings that they gave their world. Some of the cave art is located in very inaccessible places, suggesting to archeologists that the sites might have had spiritual significance—they were special, or sacred, places for ritualistic practices. Wyse and Winkleman conclude that "whatever the explanation, Paleolithic art is an outstanding and evocative monument to the full humanity achieved by the early hunters of Europe" (74). The additional conclusion is that they had a life with meaning and fulfillment. It made sense to them. And their art reflects an appreciation of this.

What this suggests is that it was the quality of their relationships with each other and the natural world, the community of life as Quinn says, that created their sense of purpose. Security, taking care of each other, being taken care of, a sense of belonging, a feeling of participation and of being needed by others, equality, contentment, personal safety, creativity, artistic expression, love, joy, peace, and wholeness—this was the cultural fabric that informed their lives and what constituted their amenities.

If we examine our own lives in the industrial world today, what do most people say when asked, "What matters most to you?" It's the same package of amenities as our ancestors—but theirs was a byproduct of their leaver ways. It's true that we moderns are able to have and appreciate these amenities. They are, however, more of a goal that we have to strive to obtain despite all of the distractions and stress that clutter our lives. When and if we get them, we appreciate them. Yet they seem frequently out of reach.

To what extent would any of us say that they are the natural byproduct of being all we can be? These values and feelings are what constitute the qualitative dimension of life. True for them as well as us. Today, it's the quantitative dimension, have all you can have, that the economy in particular concentrates on. We are left with the sense that quantity is all that matters, or that quantity equates to quality, or more often, that quality is a goal to achieve somehow independent of our quantitative fixation. Our condition today is therefore not only an aberration but one that reduces quality of life to a "struggle"—usually a very personal one. No wonder the book market is flooded with so many self-help titles. Would any of us argue that the quality of life our ancestors experienced was something for which they constantly had to struggle, along with their daily subsistence? Anthropologists have clearly said, no. Is their message simply that money doesn't buy happiness? No. It's more like, "a world driven by more-is-better works at odds with happiness."

And how about the negative feelings we experience? We have adapted perhaps too much to relationships that are demeaning, debasing, alienating, humiliating, degrading, unequal, unjust, and unfair. We continually scramble to avoid them or escape them, as they seem to be a part of modern living itself. In many respects the path of civilization and more recently that of capitalism is the path of humiliation. On the other hand, for leavers, their lives, for all of the physical hardship and lack of comfort and convenience, was a path of dignity. Why? Because they put taking care of each other ahead of getting ahead and being more. Security, equality, community, sharing and caring, and collective/cooperative labor were integral to their way. This is true for leavers today, as well.

How Did We Assimilate Be All You Can Be?

With the Agricultural Revolution humans went from a million years of being satiable survivors to becoming insatiable improvers. But this has been an evolving saga for only the last 10,000 years. The story looks like that in Figure 3.5.

Figure 3.5. A Short History of Being More

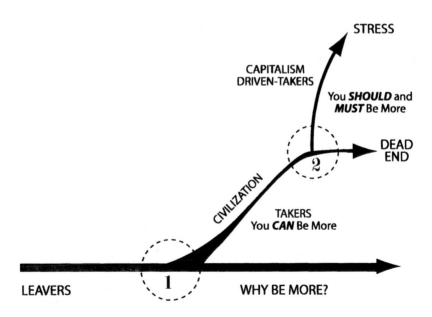

The earliest civilizations and their ruling classes understood that humans had the insatiable potential to always be more. Certainly ambition and initiative are evidenced in their expansionary and imperial conquests, in their art, and in the technical improvements they invented and commissioned. Yet in all of these civilizations, their ambition and self-interested pursuits were tempered by the overriding norm that taking care of each other was primary. This is evident, for example, in Minoan civilization in Crete around 2000 BC. Theirs was actually the origin for what later culminated in Hellenic Greece and its Golden Age, whose peak was reached around 400 BC.

The Minoans built a sophisticated palace at Knossos that included first-floor rooms with elaborate frescoes depicting flying fish, dolphins, and mass spectator events. They were clearly as luxurious as many of our contemporary counterparts. Yet the ground and basement floors contained pots and boxes filled with surplus food and other necessities stored for distribution to the commoners and slaves as needed. Wyse and Winkleman refer to this as a "flourishing redistributive economy" (140). The ruling oligarchy understood that its ambitions were subordinate to their obligations to care for the poor. As such, this didn't imply surrendering their own wealth and becoming poor themselves. But their economic behavior was not driven by the pursuit of self-interest but in the securing of their way of life. And this meant the assuring of basic necessities to all subjects. It was clearly not a competitive system driven by getting ahead. On the other hand, as we would suspect, their paternalist culture had a retarding effect on growth of all kinds compared to the dynamism of today's culture and economy.

For example, classical Greece over a thousand years later was much the same with its culture of security and paternalism. Even though they boasted an active commercial life of Mediterranean trade, markets, prices, and money—the trappings of capitalism—commerce was subordinated to traditions of art and culture and imperial security. It continued to be a self-sufficient farming economy despite its commerce. There is no evidence in their writings and philosophy that they ever imagined their purpose to be that of insatiable improvement or getting ahead. There were those on top and those on the bottom, and in fact, the crude motives of the merchants kept them from being citizens of Athens. Their status was that of "resident alien." And it was not a system of free trade, but of highly regulated and governed trade. There was no notion in any of the precapitalist civilizations that economic growth was even possible, let alone that such growth could create a rising tide to lift all boats. For these takers, and this includes more exotic examples like the Shang dynasty in the middle valley of the Yellow River (c. 3000 BC), people accepted their assigned station in life, and there was no recognition that there should be more of anything next year relative to this year. We should call the growth that did occur "embedded growth," because it was subordinated to the broader norm of taking care of each other.

For sure, harvests might be better next year due to better weather, more rain, and more land might be brought under cultivation. New irrigation and more buildings might be constructed. But they did not intentionally plan technological improvements from year to year with the hope that by doing so they could create more wealth for all. They simply were not driven by a genetic need to improve anything. Like their leaver ancestors, improvements happened more by accident than design. They evidence little understanding of how to go about intentionally creating them. "Sufficiency" guided leavers, and in precapitalist civilizations it subordinated growth, as well.

Aristotle's thoughts on this are instructive. Of course, Aristotle didn't write in a vacuum, even though he is "the last word in Hellenic speculative philosophy" (Brumbaugh 1964, 175). His mentor, Plato, stated in the *Republic* that "the insatiable desire of wealth was the...ruin of oligarchy" (Plato 1963, 275). Even pre-Socratic philosophers, like Anaximander, Thales, and the Stoics, realized that humans have a special type of being that is limitless—they knew humans could always be more tomorrow than they are today. They understood self-realization as the actualization of human potential. And they are right. But what they concluded was that to pursue this insatiably was not the path of virtue and happiness. They cautioned against the *insatiable* pursuit of anything, in fact. Aristotle followed their train of thought. He knew that human desire was insatiable and that wealth and greed were, too. He admonished against the excessive pursuit of wealth, suggesting that satiability, sufficiency, and moderation—his Golden Mean—were a wiser choice (Aristotle 1982, 431-443). The power of choice, and the free will from which it stems, were the key human qualities necessary for obtaining the good life.

For Aristotle, being all one could be was not the secret to happiness. Instead, one should choose to do the right thing when ethical and moral dilemmas presented themselves—this was the way to live. As David Korten states, "The ruthless pursuit of personal material advantage that modern economists consider normal, Aristotle would have judged pathological and destructive of both self and civility of society" (Korten 1999, 140). So these early civilizations, by their written record, suggest that being and having more are possible, yet are not the right choice for living the good life.

They understood that creativity and imagination are the traits that fuel artistic expression and that through them we can get a glimpse of perfection. What concerned them was the human trait for insatiability, and they were not about to make a virtue of it. Aristotle viewed the youth of his civilization as having insatiable appetites, suggesting that they "err by doing things in excess or more intensely, they love too much, they hate too much, and likewise with all other things" (Aristotle 1982, 625). Our freedom culture today is driven by insatiability and suggests that it need only be channeled into productive activities to be a virtue. The momentum of the be all you can be culture was only beginning to build in Aristotle's day. But he would have lost both the battle and the war against it.

Subsequently, Hellenic Greece gave way to Rome. The cultural norms of satiability, taking care of each other, and sufficiency did not change. Seneca, a Stoic philosopher and advisor to the Roman emperor, Nero (*reg.* 49–62 AD), echoed Aristotle. Seneca cautioned against the pursuit of wealth, saying that you will only learn from such things to crave still greater. Natural desires are limited; but those which spring from false opinion can have no stopping-point. When you are traveling on a road, there must be an end; but when astray, your wanderings are limitless. Recall your steps, therefore, from idle things, and when you would know whether that which you seek is based upon a natural or upon a misleading desire, consider whether it can stop at any definite point. If you find, after having traveled far, that there is a more distant goal always in view, you may be sure that this condition is contrary to nature (Seneca 1967, 108-9).

It's ironic that today's conventional wisdom suggests just the opposite— "insatiable is good, if focused effectively towards being and having more, and it's consistent with our nature." Like Aristotle, Seneca lost the battle and the war, as well.

The next group of thinkers in the progression toward the 16th century is the Christian scholars. Rome became Christian under Theodosius in 381 and St. Augustine was one of its first theologians. He was a pagan who converted to Christianity and became part of the growing movement of Christian ascetics— those that renounced materialism as a means to cleanse their faith. St. Augustine asserted that faith, belief in Jesus as the Savior, is the key to salvation.

He rejected insatiability of any kind believing that minimalism and an "other-worldly" focus provide the discipline necessary for being saved. Being all one can be did not gel with his theology. "From his personal experiences Augustine concluded that bodily appetites distract from the contemplation of God. He denounced as sinful, therefore, even the simplest of physical pleasures" (Greer 1972, 105). In this respect, not much changed for a thousand years in Europe. St. Thomas Aquinas (1225–1274) carried on the satiable and faith-based theology of Augustine. In *Summa Theologica*, Aquinas insists that "virtue denotes a determinate perfection of a power," suggesting that finding God through reason (that the Greeks emphasized) grounded in faith is based on *per habitus*— good habits (Davies 1992, 240). A "determinate" perfection of a power meant to him a very satiable practice of faith-driven habits. It was not about being more tomorrow than one is today, not about an endless quest to find God in one's soul. He, too, like his predecessors, didn't associate being more as a virtue.

What Figure 3.5 suggests is that between points One and Two, precapitalist civilizations were constrained in their growth and development of both the individual and the society by a culture that put obligations to God and others ahead of self-actualization. "You can be more" as stated in Figure 3.5 does not mean one is allowed to be more; it means that humans have the ability to be more. The prevailing cultural norms recognized that being more was possible but cautioned against it.

Capitalism: You Should and Must Be More

Both the culture and economy changed dramatically with the 16th century. The Renaissance, the scientific revolution, the Enlightenment, and capitalism brought it about. This unusual series of events led by thinkers like Descartes, Newton, and Bacon on the one hand, and Hobbes, Locke, and Hume on the other, linked scientific inquiry/method with the elevation of the individual to "superhuman-with-inalienable rights," and finally to the notion that self-actualization is the best way to personal happiness and social improvement. Science gave humans a new sense for control and domination of the natural world. It was an uninhibited ego booster.

The individual was about to achieve an unprecedented level of technical command over life that could not help but ratchet economic growth to unparalleled heights. Now it was clearly possible that all people could be more. There was enough growth to universalize the be all you can be possibility. And in the context of the new market system that relied on individual self-interest, people could, should, and must be free to go about getting ahead. The market made people insecure, stripped away the old traditions of caring for one another, and clarified the extent to which individual pursuit of self-development and greed could be reconciled with a more fully developed society. It all fit.

Science brought technology and growth, but only if the individual could be unleashed from the bonds of the old ways. Growth made it possible for all people to be more, and they would be compelled to be more, if security was no longer assured. And they could do this if they had individual freedom. The epiphanal message was that being all one could be is good. It begets everything good—more life, a higher standard of living, stronger people, more enlightened people, and it's insatiable. It quickly became clear that more economic growth would foster more personal and social growth, which would bring about more economic growth, and so on—a mutually reinforcing and self-reproducing trajectory of progress. Of course, it would otherwise be advisable to encourage or demand that people be more and self-develop, but with capitalism the incentive to do so was built into the system itself. "You're on your own; go make something of yourself—or else."

In a remarkably brief span of 200 hundred years, the be all you can be value became a moral and economic imperative. Among Francis Bacon's (1561–1626) many achievements as a scientist and philosopher, not the least of them is his pioneering argument that the value of science is that it is the best instrument that humans have to control nature for their own improvement. "The new science was not just an academic or intellectual enterprise to increase man's knowledge of nature; its purpose was to give man mastery over nature, a mastery that would enable man to transform the quality of his life on earth" (Cranston 1967, 236). In *Novum Organum* (1620), Bacon's seminal work, he stated that science could "enlarge the bounds of human empire to the affecting of all things possible" (Rifkin 2004, 99). Bacon was a philosopher of productvism, but he was only the first of many. His ideas were radical at the time, because before him there was not only less interest in science but it was embedded by the culture of security. Curiosity about the natural world and an interest in understanding it were common to all of the earlier civilizations, and as much as Bacon's statement is a passionately accurate symbol of takerism, it took modern science and capitalism to reveal the drive that lay dormant in the taker way.

Harnessing nature through science and then extending human understanding by way of it, created a new interest in education. This is partly due to the fact that with education, people could more effectively self-actualize and develop their insatiable potential. And education not only became the favored vehicle for this, but with the new individual freedom and economic growth it could be universalized—extended to all humans. Previously, education was valued as a voice of wisdom enhancing the ability of the ruling elites to govern the world more gracefully. Over the last 300 hundred years education has become even more the preferred means to greater self- and social-development.

Today we see it as *the* ticket for being all we can be, and it is insatiable, as the phrases "life long learning" and "continuous learning" suggest. John Amos Comenius (1592–1670), was one of the first to articulate the value of education for its own sake. In his classic, *The Great Didactic* (1632), written when he was bishop of the Moravian Church, he noted the connection between education and insatiable self-improvement. In 1668 in a treatise drafted for the Royal Society of London, he said "philosophy brought to perfection" would "exhibit the true and distinctive qualities of things for the constantly progressive increase of all that makes for good to mind, body, and estate" (Ulich 1967, 147).

In the 20th century this idea was refined by the socialist, John Dewey (1859–1952), one of the founders of America's only original philosophy, pragmatism, and an icon of contemporary philosophy of education. In his 1916 book, *Democracy and Education*, he states, "When it is said that education is development, everything depends on *how* development is conceived. Our net conclusion is that life is development, and that developing, growing, is life" (Frankena

1965, 20). The fact that Dewey was a socialist has little to do with his belief, like Comenius, that self-development is an end-in-itself and to the extent that education is a means to this, it is an end-in-itself, as well. But Dewey was by no means the first socialist to embrace the imperative of productivism and be all you can be. Karl Marx (1818–1883) preceded him a century earlier.

The 19th century witnessed the maturation of capitalism through the great achievements of the Industrial Revolution. It was also the century in which be all you can be became both an economic imperative and a moral and social one—you should and must be more. Both Marx and the British utilitarian, John Stuart Mill (1806–1873), are illustrative in this respect. They were contemporaries but on opposite sides of the political fence.

Marx was surely the most original and comprehensive critic of capitalism, while Mill was one of its staunchest defenders. But what makes them the same is their mutual belief in be all you can be. They were uncommonly vocal in their defense of productivism. Marx's guiding principle for the critique of capitalism was the "full and free development of the individual." And like Marx, Mill argued for the "fullness of life."

In his classic statement on individual freedom, *On Liberty* (1859), Mill maintained that the best path to continuous social development was that which gave the individual the most liberty to pursue his or her self-development. The path of liberty was, for Mill, capitalism. Why? Because as we take for granted today, capitalism does the most with personal freedom of any system yet established. He said, "It is only the cultivation of individuality which produces, or can produce, well-developed human beings…for what more or better can be said of any condition of human affairs than that it brings human beings themselves nearer to the best thing they can be?" (Mill, 128). Marx agreed.

In Marx's *Early Manuscripts* (1844) he criticized capitalism for the inherent inequality it created. The inequality he was talking about was not so much wealth distribution as the inequality in access to individual self-development. The rich were able to do lots of self-actualizing and pursue being more, because they had money and means. The poor and working class were stuck selling their labor, toiling all day at alienating jobs, and had little income with which to further their own self-development. Socialism, he felt, would be the first system to allow all of humanity the opportunity to equally be all they could be. With socialism and then communism, Marx stated, "it will be seen how in place of the wealth and poverty of political economy [capitalism] come the rich human being and rich human need. The rich human being is simultaneously the human being in need of the totality of life activities—the man in whom his own realization exists as an inner necessity, as need" (Marx 1978, 9). Of course, the individual rich in needs is one who has internalized be all you can be ("inner necessity") and is an insatiable self-developer. How "rich" can we be in our need to develop ourselves? Infinitely rich. That's the difference between rich in money that capitalism touts and rich in self-development that socialism is supposed to create.

Both Marx and Mill shared the value that life is about insatiable development. They both shared the belief in the individual. Mill saw all of this as possible within capitalism, while Marx said that it required radical overhaul of capitalism—socialism.

Our conclusion that being leftwing or rightwing makes no difference when it comes to the shared imperative of productivism is as true today as it was then. There have been very few critics of capitalism from the left who haven't been believers in social- and self-development. The issue for the last two hundred years has been mainly about which kind of system will work best to foster our self-actualization. But to criticize the idea of self-actualization? It's not been a popular conversation. What this amounts to is that the debate between the left and right over capitalism has been confined to the inner circle of Figure 2.1. Social criticism has rarely extended to the outer circle of our be all you can be culture. The debate has been primarily about whether assured security or earned security is the best motivator.

By the 1950s, the imperative that we are all supposed to continually be more was thoroughly assimilated. We no longer thought to question the belief that humans are reducible to insatiable self-actualizers. In 1968 Abraham Maslow published *Toward a Psychology of Being*, where he argued that humans face a hierarchy of psychological needs from the lowest of safety to the highest of self-actualization. These needs are not socially induced, he says, but are intrinsic and part of our essence—our human nature. In a classic statement that both Marx and Mill would endorse, Maslow says, "Man demonstrates in his own nature a pressure toward fuller and fuller Being, more and more perfect actualization of his humanness in exactly the same naturalistic, scientific sense that an acorn may be said to be 'pressing toward' being an oak tree" (Maslow, 160). How full of self-actualization can we get? That's like asking, "How much potential do I have?" As far as we know, it's unlimited. To suggest that we have reached the point in the 21st century when many are now full would be like telling a teacher that we can't learn more because our brains are unfortunately filled up.

The idea that we *can* be more is all too true. The fixation that we *should* and *must* be always more is not. What our history tells us is that Maslow was wrong. Humans haven't always been driven by the biological or genetic need to be more, because such a need is not engineered in our human nature. Our ancestors weren't insatiable improvers. It's a cultural and evolutionary development that we've grown to accept as natural. Being more is a choice for humanity rather an intrinsic imperative. Our culture and our economy drive us to always be more, and do so in such an effective and efficient manner that we think it's us who are doing the driving. We're victims of a cultural imperative that no one has told us about.

Part Four

Save the World to Save Yourself

The Personal and the Political

We've been examining the culture and the economic system that drive us—compel us—to always be more. It's vital at this point to reemphasize something: it's time to take the drive out of the system and culture, so that you can be free to self-develop or not. There is nothing in what I'm arguing that suggests that a more sustainable and satiable future requires that you surrender this freedom. People do have the capacity to insatiably self-actualize. No dispute there. And as individuals, many of us have talents and capacities that we want to improve and develop. That's fine. But a system with cultural coercive power to force more out of us should be rethought. That's what we are doing.

Our goal is to create a culture and economy that works efficiently and smoothly but doesn't cause us to always be on the consumerist-performance treadmill. To get off the treadmill today is not easy. To drop out of the mainstream is not easy. But it should be. To stay on the treadmill of productivism is not easy. It's a big source of stress and anxiety. If we hop off to reduce our stress, we are swimming upstream, and that ends up being stressful as well—unless you have lots of money. The problem, as we know, is that first we have to be successful productivists in order to earn the money. That may or may not be an option for many of us. Winning the lottery or substantial inheritance can help, but still—not an option for most of us.

At the personal level you face stress, anxiety, being frantic and overwhelmed, fearful and insecure, desperate, depressed, and despairing—a lot of negative psychological and emotional states. The purpose of capitalism is not to create stress free living, except to the extent that you can compete so effectively that you become a financial winner in this game—and it's usually at some one else's expense. It's a system of winners and losers after all. Don't kid yourself. If everyone earned a college degree, we'd end up with a glutted college degreed market with most of us being underemployed. One might argue, on the other hand, that stress-free living is supposed to be a byproduct of a higher standard of living. And capitalism is a wealth-producing machine, so successful productivism on your part should get you above or beyond the stress threshold. It doesn't seem to be working that way for many people. That's why it's called a treadmill. And that's what Mill was getting at a hundred years ago when he said that there hasn't been a technological innovation that has ever saved us any toil. How high does the standard of living have to be? Clearing the bar sounds good but it's difficult when our culture keeps raising it.

At the political—that is, the "system" and "culture" level—things are a bit different. You suffer stress while the system is on its way to destroying the habitability of the planet. The stress you endure simply assures that the system will go on destroying the earth, all the while trying to convince you that the goods life is the good life. None of what's happening is one-dimensional. There are tensions at work, instead. You have stress, but you also have good times and a decent standard of living—at least for some. Some have stress and live poor, too. On the other hand, at the political level capitalism is destroying the planet but also churning out more stuff. The point is to get a better grip on the multiple tensions that continually keep us confused. Marx told workers in 1848 that they had nothing to lose but their chains. Even workers fifty years later realized that it's not that simple. It's complex. And it's only more so today. So it takes awhile to figure out what's really going on so that we can sort out what's salvageable from what needs to be chucked.

The World Needs to be Saved

If we suspend our examination of your personal problems for a bit, we can look at how they dovetail with the major global issues of our time, not the least of which is growing inequality, environmental crisis, and violence. This is the political level. Edward Abbey once said, "Today, our technological-industrial social machine is trying to enslave the whole of Nature—put everything to work for the sake of human greed and human power. That, I think, is the ultimate evil of the modern age" (Lim 2002, 67). He was clearly talking about capitalism, but he, too, realized that it is more than capitalism that's at issue. By "technological-industrial social machine" he was inferring that capitalism itself is part of a bigger cultural web, like Figure 2.1 suggests. And capitalism is clearly a machine. It's based on an *extractive* model of life and nature.

Capitalism is an extractive system. That's also another way to talk about takerism—to take is to extract. It wants to extract, is compelled to extract, as much as possible from workers, from nature, from the stock of natural resources, from the carrying capacity of the planet itself, and from your own being. To pursue the have all you can have consumerist smorgasbord, it must be extractive. Yet the be all you can be imperative of today's culture is extractive as well. You are supposed to extract as much as you possibly can from that untapped potential that you carry around in your being. Presumably then, idleness is waste, is bad; extraction is good, is productive.

But the world needs to be saved because it is about to be destroyed by overuse. What has happened? With capitalism our be all you can be self-actualizing gets channeled into the have all you can have economy. The obsession with having more is wreaking havoc with the earth's recuperative powers. The ideology of capitalism says that the good life is the goods life. It also *directs our energy* into having more as compensation for work, being more on the job, and productivism in general. There is now fairly widespread agreement that having all you can have is destroying the earth.

The key to both your personal fulfillment and saving the planet is this: *the insatiable desire to have more—that's destroying the planet—is a result of the insatiable desire to be more.* It's not hard to make the connection that the have all you can have ideology is causing biospheric overuse. It's a bit more complicated to argue that this is caused by our obsession with being more. And as we've said, reeling in our consumerist behaviors is easier than letting go of the being-more idea.

Could capitalism exist and function effectively without the fixation on always having more stuff? Not likely. Businesses are driven by maximizing profits as this takes place within a competitive struggle. If you don't, your competitor might, and you lose. They need to expand to survive. They need ever more consumers, and they need to have us buying as much as we possibly can. They need us to have insatiable wants and the ideology of more is better and shop 'til you drop. They want us to find happiness through buying either things or experiences (Rifkin 2000). They would like to see life become a "paid-for experience," as Rifkin argues.

This gets complicated in part because there are many ways to be more and actualize our insatiable potential that don't involve having more stuff. It is conceivable that as a culture, we might reach a consensus or critical turning point, when we say, "Buying and owning things just doesn't do it for me anymore." And we might begin a shift away from satisfying nonmaterial needs with material commodities—that is, the market—to being more spiritual and so on. We might begin to actualize our potential in ways that don't involve buying in the market.

This is not a transition that businesses are likely to encourage. In fact, if Rifkin's hypothesis in *The Age of Access* is correct, if we say that we want to improve our musical talents, read more, take more walks, be closer to nature, have more community, and improve our ability to love, be virtuous, a better friend, and partner or parent, it is in businesses' interest to find a way to own those experiences and then sell them to us. In this respect, we would no longer be buying things as a surrogate for love and affection, but we would still be reliant on the market for love and affection *experiences*. In other words, if we choose continuing to pursue be all we can be but *not* have all you can have, we might save the earth. But businesses will not sponsor this and will, in fact, try to find a way to make us dependent upon them for being all we can be. They will try to find ways to sell us either self-actualizing experiences or the means we need to obtain them. Their need is to extract. Of course, what they are looking for is for you to want to extract as much as possible from yourself (by way of self-development) and be reliant on them for help.

The concept of a be all you can be society that is not have all you can have is gaining popularity with the voluntary simplicity movements and the post-materialist movement in Europe. Be more without having more? Is there a way to do this and still take the "drive" out of the system? And have a system that still functions well? Is there a way to do this without continuing to measure one

another by achievements and accomplishments? Can we go beyond productivism, in other words, and still retain the value, at least individually and privately,
of insatiable self-actualization? It's possible, but first we have to recognize the
destructive trajectory that capitalism and its globalization are on.

Consumerist Catastrophe

Ed Ayres, in *God's Last Offer: Negotiating for a Sustainable Future* (1999), makes the case that there are four "spikes"—"megaphenomena"—that "represent dangers of a magnitude that is hard to convey without seeming to lapse into hyperbole" (Ayres, 10). These four trends fairly well summarize the catastrophic trajectory that the have all you can have economy is on. There's carbon dioxide (CO_2), population, species extinction, and consumption, all of which, as our scientific data show, are spiking today. All of them point to one event: overuse of planetary carrying capacity. The CO_2 spike indicates not only global warming but pollution from a carbon-based industrial growth machine. All the while, human population growth is not only out of control but is driving other species in the community of life to rates of extinction that are over a thousand times as fast as evolution creates. Finally, there is the consumption spike, which together with population growth means a double whammy. More people are one thing, but a doubling of human population in the last fifty years coupled with a seven-fold increase in output is obviously not sustainable. The earth can tolerate more people or more stuff but not both, as we know. The spikes resemble Figure 4.1. Things are reasonably sustainable for humankind until the watershed of driven-takerism in the 16th century—the economy of insatiable improvers.

Figure 4.1. The Consequences of Have All You Can Have

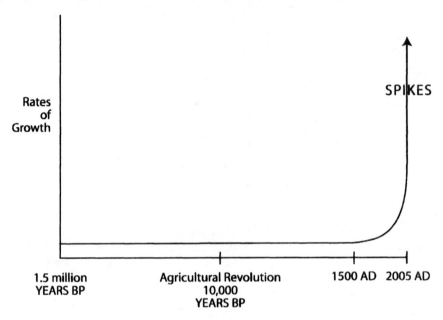

The World Watch Institute's *State of the World 2004* is instructive. Looking at global consumption, on the one hand, suggests that it is both out of control and extremely unequal. The United States and Canada are 5.2 percent of world population but account for 31.5 percent of its private consumption. If we add to this the consumption spending of Western Europe, with their 6.4 percent of world population and 28.7 percent of consumer spending, we find 11.6 percent of the world consuming over 60 percent of its resources. Yet South Asia has 22.4 percent of global population but consumes only 2 percent of its output (Gardner, Assadourian, and Sarin 2004, 6). And then there is China with the highest average economic growth rates in the world over the last decade and allocating wealth to over a sixth of the world's population. Every day in 2003 there was an additional 11,000 new cars on their streets. If car sales continue, it is expected that there will be 150 million cars in China by 2015—exceeding the U.S. total by 18 million (3). Of course China is not part of this statistic: the richest fifth of the world owns 80 percent of all the cars. But they aspire to be. And it's not only more but bigger: new houses in the United States in 2002 were 38 percent bigger than in 1975 (4).

The spike in global consumption is merely the tip of the iceberg. Because what's important for planetary carrying capacity are the *consequences* of our high mass consumption. Global use of coal, oil, and natural gas was almost five times greater in 2002 than fifty years earlier. More than half of the world's wetlands have been lost due to draining or filling for agriculture and settlement by humans. We've doubled our use of wood since 1950 and more than half of the world's forests have been cut down. Sea level due to climate change has risen 10-20 centimeters in the last century. In the last fifty years the world fish catch has increased almost five-fold, and industrial fleets have fished out 90 percent of tuna, marlin, swordfish, sharks, cod, halibut, and flounder (Gardner, Assadourian, and Sarin 2004, 17). Water demand has tripled in the last fifty years, as well. Water tables have begun falling in China, India, and the United States, which together account for about half of the world's grain production (Brown 2003, 9). This is a consequence of the fact that grain demand has tripled since 1950.

Overpumping of our global water tables is quite likely the best kept secret of the immanent ecological crisis. We can overpump for an unknown period, keeping the water flowing, 70 percent of it for irrigation, and continue to meet our food needs. But water tables continue to fall. Eventually we have drained aquifers—many now have been—and the "food bubble" economies burst. Lester Brown's *Plan B: Rescuing a Planet under Stress and a Civilization in Trouble* (2003) is an engaging read that exposes this. In his words, "The world is moving into uncharted territory as human demands override the sustainable yield of natural systems" (Brown 2003, 19). The "ecological footprint" is a good way to understand overuse. Redefining Progress, a California-based, sustainability organization, has estimated that the earth has about 1.9 hectares of land (4-5 acres) per person available for providing resources and absorbing our waste.

Yet the average person today is using 2.3 hectares. And the distribution of productive resources is extremely skewed. The average American uses 9.7 hectares, while a Mozambican uses only .47. "Footprint analysis shows that total consumption levels had already exceeded the planet's ecological capacity by the late 1970s or early 1980s. Such overconsumption is possible only by drawing down stocks of resource reserves, as when wellwater is pumped to the point that groundwater levels decrease" (Gardner, Assadourian, and Sarin 2004, 16-17). We are so far into the overuse crisis that is only made worse by the inequality that accompanies it. Two hundred years ago, with the beginning of the Industrial Revolution and only a billion people, no one would have thought to talk about overconsumption and overuse. A system like capitalism that promised more of everything imaginable, also promised it to more people. Growth was seen as a universal cure for the social problems associated with inequality, since such a solution was politically palatable to the rich. Thus, the poor can have more without requiring anything from the rich.

Inequality: Compounding the Earth Crisis

There are essentially two enormous issues facing humanity: the environmental crisis of overuse (consumerism) and inequality—mostly a result of social injustice. Since the purpose of capitalism has never been to create a more equal world or a more socially just one, our dominant ideology has insisted that as a wealth machine it can create enough additional output for everyone that none need suffer. Whenever called to defend the system, conservatives have for two hundred years responded that growth is the palliative. We are only now beginning to recognize 1) global economic growth is worsening inequality, and 2) such growth isn't sustainable anyway.

There are 2.8 billion people, almost half the world population that live on less than $2 a day—what the World Bank and UN say is necessary to meet minimum material needs. They are poor, and their numbers have increased by 50 percent since 1980 (Shah 2005, 1). If we exclude China, whose incomes have quadrupled in the last 25 years, the world is becoming poorer—global poverty is increasing. There are about 1.2 billion people who are categorized as "extremely poor" since they live—just barely—on less than a dollar a day, and the World Bank suggests their numbers are growing (Gardner, Assadourian, and Sarin 2004, 6). In 2002 the UN stated that there are 840 million people who are undernourished, adding that in ten years of global economic growth during the 1990s, this number decreased by only 2.5 million per year. In the 2002 report they concluded: "thus we must report that progress has virtually ground to a halt" (8).

In 59 of the poorest nations, average income is lower today than 20 years ago, according to the UN *Human Development Report* of 1999. By the end of the 1990s, about 1.6 billion people were economically worse off than 15 years earlier. The globalization of capitalism isn't helping, as UNCTAD reported in 1999 that the world's poorest nations' share of world trade declined by more than 40 percent since 1980.

The World Health Organization has stated that there is no precedent for today's inequality in which the richest 1.2 billion are overnourished and overweight, while the poorest 1.2 billion are undernourished and underweight. Almost a billion adults are illiterate. Eight thousand a day are dying of AIDS in Africa, lowering the life expectancy in sub-Saharan Africa from 62 to 47 (Brown 2003, 5). Consequently, by 2010 there is estimated to be about 20 million AIDS orphans in sub-Saharan Africa. There are over a billion people who lack safe drinking water and 2.4 billion live in villages or urban squatter settlements without sewage facilities.

There are other ways to measure the extent to which the rich are getting richer as the poor get poorer. The World Bank has announced that the gap between the poorest third and richest third of humanity is increasing, while the share of the middle third has also dropped. But this pattern isn't new. "The average income in the richest 20 countries is now 37 times that in the poorest 20. This ratio has doubled in the past 40 years, mainly because of lack of growth in the poorest countries" (*World Development Report 2003*, 2). The ratio of the richest fifth of the world to that of the poorest fifth increased from 30:1 in 1960 to 82:1 in 1995 (Schnitzer 2000, 370). The richest one percent in the world actually owns as much wealth and consumes as many resources as the poorest half of the world's six billion people (Atwood and Barnett 2004, A3). In the United States, the gap between rich and poor is growing, as well. It has the worst distribution of wealth and income of any industrial nation. The richest one percent has more income than the poorest 40 percent, and this gap is the widest we've seen in 70 years (Global Issues 2005). It's only getting worse here and everywhere else today.

Growth is not ameliorating poverty and it's not lessening inequality. Yet those who suffer from economic hardship and deprivation of material necessities are constantly barraged with the images of the goods life and told to keep striving for the have all you can have dream. The Chinese have been the most successful. But most of the world's poor are left out of the loop of "free" trade. The UN states that poor nations lose about $2 billion a day due to unfair trade rules. That's 14 times what they receive in foreign aid! The 49 nations that are the poorest 10 percent of global population account for only 0.4 percent of world trade, less than a twentieth of their share. And this is worsening, as well (UNCTAD 2001).

Inequality and the environmental crisis? These are the two critical dramas that will make or break a sustainable future. They are both social crises related to the system's efforts to keep pumping the have all you can have message. Not all of the inequality can be blamed on capitalism alone, as its origins are with civilization and takerism 10,000 years ago. But today as it rears its ugly head and people at the bottom of the global hierarchy of power and wealth act out with rage, violence, and terror, the system's only response is to caution patience and offer a measure of trickle-down growth. None of which is working. The environmental crisis is more straightforward. Its link to capitalism is more obvious. Even children in our public schools have gotten the idea that the pollution and overuse that threaten the earth are related to the issue of growth and our fixation with "more." Perhaps it is not an inordinate leap for them to connect this with our economic system at some point. But there is a variety of blinders that operate on all of us.

For one thing, there are two types of inequality, but only one of them is in the mainstream conversation. The one we hear about the most is the inequality that results from the fact that the world has different endowments of resources in different regions. We are told that some regions and continents are poor in resources, water, arable land, climate, and so on. These regions or nations within them are poor because they lack the adequate and sufficient resources to develop themselves out of poverty. Other nations, like the United States, are rich in resources and have ambitious people who make the most of them. They get rich, while the others fall behind. Therefore, the inequality is due to differing circumstances and endowments, possibly some extenuating historical legacies, like colonialism, as well. Walter Rostow (1916–2003), the advisor to President Kennedy and architect of the Vietnam War wrote his development classic, *The Stages of Economic Growth: An Anti-Communist Manifesto* (1960), with such an argument. Their point is obvious: don't blame the haves of the world for the inequality. It's not their doing. There's no exploitation going on to cause it.

The other type of inequality is what Marx explained. In this case the inequality between the haves and have-nots is the result of a structural relationship: the poverty of the one is caused by exploitation and injustice by the other. The poor are poor because the rich have plundered and pillaged the resources that formerly belonged to the have-nots, or the rich have asserted control over their subjects in such a way as to exploit their labor, make them pay a tribute, extract a surplus, and keep the oppressed victims in a state of unequal dependency.

With the first form of inequality, there is no structural relationship between haves and have-nots. The inequality is no one's fault. In which case, if the poor want to be better off and reduce the degree of inequality that separates them from the rich, they can only make a moral appeal to the rich for some form of redistribution of wealth, resources, or power. The rich are in a situation where they can say yes, or no, to the appeal. Such an appeal has nothing to do with injustice. The poor can complain and ask for help or aid, but that's it. The rich can politely refuse, saying that it is none of their concern. Or they can say yes, on the basis that we are all one human family knowing that "there but for the grace of God go I."

With the other type of inequality, the poor can blame the rich for having made them poor. This is a case of injustice, exploitation, and an undemocratic relationship of subordination. The have-nots, rather than making a moral appeal to the kindness and generosity of the rich, can *demand* redistribution. Their demand is based on the principle of democracy. An injustice has been done. They are entangled in an unfair relationship of dependency in which they are being cheated out of what should be their resources. Or they lack democratic control over the use of their own labor. If they have been forced off of the land, thrust into urban slums, and then compelled to sell their labor to the highest bidder, they have a case for redistribution of power due to this injustice.

Increasingly, the have-nots of the world, many of whom are in the Southern Hemisphere, have decided that their inequality is not of the first type, but of the second. We see this issue raised at the World Social Forum today. A study of their history since the 16th century, and a careful examination of their relationship to the North, the developed nations, and transnational corporations serving the North, has led them to believe that today's inequality is a structural relationship of injustice. Some of it stems from the legacies of colonialism and imperialism, but much of it exists from their current relationship to the global economy and its corporations. In other words, the have-nots were once victims of an unjust relationship of colonialism, and they still are today—except they don't use the word, colonial, but instead talk about it as unequal dependency.

The relation of injustice continues. The more the have-nots see it this way, the more unstable the world will be. The more convinced they are that this is the case and the less effective appeals to the rich become, the more desperate the have-nots become, and the more violent their efforts at redistribution of power and their struggle for justice. The global social divide is quite apparent to those in the UN. President Bush maintains that both the poor and rich nations have a common enemy in terrorism, but the poor nations have been arguing in the General Assembly that poverty is the biggest threat to their security. "Although sympathetic to these security challenges, poor nations believe that their safety is most compromised not by terrorism but by debilitating poverty" (Atwood and Barnett 2004, A3). If economic growth was solving the problem of inequality or lifting the bottom rungs of the economic ladder upward, it would be less worrisome. But it's not.

Whether or not the rich want to hear the message of the have-nots, they will be forced to deal with it. Maybe today's inequality is of both types. There are plenty of historians and political scientists who agree with the injustice perspective (Wolfe 1997, Korten 1999, Chomsky 2003). And some who don't. But the point for us is that this should be *the* debate both within and between nations. It should be the number one item on the public agenda, along with the environmental crisis.

Das Bogans

Today's inequality and environmental crisis are for the first time in human history truly global phenomena. The scale of the global economy would have been unfathomable even fifty years ago. Words like behemoth and juggernaut simply don't capture it. Fifty-one of the 100 largest economies in the world are corporations. And the top 500 multinationals account for 70 percent of global trade, and this percentage has been steadily increasing for twenty years (CorpWatch 2005). Much of the "Super-size Me" activity is a result of the compete-or-die struggle in the global economy. The more clout a firm has in the international market the better it can stay afloat and grow—which it needs to do to survive.

Proctor and Gamble announced in January 2005, that it is positioned to take over Gillette for $57 billion dollars. It stated that this was necessary in order to expand its overseas sales. This merger would make P&G the world's largest consumer-products company, creating "a behemoth with more than $60 billion in revenues" (Sutel 2005, A8). Their strategy, the company said, is to penetrate markets in both China and Eastern Europe. Gillette's CEO, James M. Kilts told analysts that "we believe we can bring these companies together and create a juggernaut," mentioning that, "I'm a great believer in scale," and that such a consolidation is better than "getting stuck with the leftovers" (A8). U.S. companies began 2005 with an excess of over a trillion dollars in cash and embarking on a wave of mergers not seen since the hostile-takeover days of the 1980s.

"The Gillette-P&G deal is part of a 'new wave' coming as firms seek growth in a global economy," states Ron Scherer of the *Christian Science Monitor*, adding that "the supersizing of American business is accelerating" (Scherer 2005, D1). The magnitude of these numbers is more than most of us can comprehend. President Bush sent his federal budget to Congress a month after the Gillette-P&G announcement, asking for $2.5 trillion. This, despite the fact that it doesn't include the $1 billion being spent each week for the military occupation of Iraq! And the government budget is only 20 percent of the annual $12 trillion output of the U.S. economy.

Spending comparisons can help give us a sense for size. For example, the wealthy of the world spend $18 billion on makeup and cosmetics, while for only $12 billion we could provide reproductive health care for all of the world's women. European and Americans spend $17 billion a year on pet food, which would be enough to eliminate world hunger and malnutrition. With the $15 billion spent on perfume, we could assure universal literacy *and* provide clean drinking water for everyone (Gardner, Assadourian, and Sarin 2004, 10).

In 1970 when Michael Harrington (1928–1989), an icon of America's 20th century socialist movement, said that capitalism is "an intricate system of antagonistic cooperation," he captured a tension in capitalism that surely has much to do with its dynamism (Harrington 1970, 3). The antagonism is that of competition, while the cooperation is that between the "voluntary" choice of workers to sell their labor, consumers to buy products, and firms to buy and sell both. As people continue to play this game, with or without stress and anxiety, the system will forge ahead on its contradictory path of wealth and destruction.

Another way to think of capitalism is that it is an organized system of irresponsibility. It's a bogan system. "Bogan" is Australian street-slang for "loser." It's commonly heard by teenage women when referring to boyfriends they no longer like. Of course, with a colloquialism such as bogan, there is no precise definition. While living in Australia a number of years ago, the term never meant much. My daughter was in high school, so I heard the word frequently from her friends. Then a few years ago I began to reconsider the word, realizing that it captured more than "loser." It suggests the idea of being unaware and irresponsible. And there is, unfortunately, a more severe form of boganism: uncaring and irresponsible. In effect there are those who are unaware and therefore irresponsible, and then there are those who actually are aware but don't care, and are then irresponsible.

The unaware type are "little bogans," while the uncaring type are "big bogans." As we rethink our culture of insatiable freedom and our economy of insatiable improvers, perhaps it will occur to you, as it did me, that we live in a bogan economy. It's one of organized irresponsibility, some of which is due to lack of awareness of consequences—little boganism—and some of which results from not caring about the consequences—big boganism.

Most defenders of capitalism, for example Nobel Laureate, Milton Friedman in his classic *Capitalism and Freedom* (1962), emphasize that it is an organized system of *individual responsibility*. This is true of Ayn Rand's individualist/libertarian philosophy articulated in books like *Atlas Shrugged* (1957) and *The Fountainhead* (1943). In fact, the home page for the Ayn Rand Institute quotes her: "My philosophy, in essence, is the concept of man as a heroic being, with his own happiness as the moral purpose of his life, with productive achievement as his noblest activity and reason as his only absolute" (Ayn Rand Institute). Not only does her remark suggest personal responsibility for one's life (find and make your own happiness) but also proudly touts the moral imperative of our culture: the purpose of a human life is to insatiably develop it—"be all you can be is all that matters."

Even President Bush's call for the "ownership society" implies as much. The conservative belief that capitalism is organized responsibility means that you need to take responsibility for your own life, your own happiness, your own needs, and ultimately, your own security. This is merely another way of saying to us, "you're on your own, pal. Sink or swim. Compete or die. Earn your security by exercising your freedom. In doing so you'll be all you can be." And more importantly, by each individual taking responsibility for his or her life in our market economy, the general interest of all will be best served. Stated differently, "pursue your own self-interest, be responsible for yourself, and all will be well for you *and the society*." This is what Adam Smith meant by the invisible hand: being responsible for yourself will further the common interest of society.

If this is so, how can we claim the opposite: capitalism is organized irresponsibility? Because in our competitive market system, the focus is clearly on you being responsible for *your life only*. The invisible hand is supposed to do the rest. Thus, competition will allow you to restrict you responsibility to yourself and simultaneously reconcile that with the general needs of our society. The problem is, and this is what makes it a bogan economy, that by being responsible for yourself, you don't have to be responsible for any of the collectively-created consequences, like global warming, population growth, environmental destruction, overconsumption, inequality, and species extinction. David Korten states that "Capitalism's beguiling promise of freedom and prosperity *without* the commensurate burden of responsibility is perhaps the primary source of its deadly attraction" (Korten 1999, 137). You can do what you want, take care of yourself, be more and have more, without having to address or take responsibility for the *social* consequences. Capitalism says to us, "Think about yourself." It doesn't admonish us to think about consequences. The difference is that between individual responsibility and social responsibility. The former is mandated by the system: "be responsible for your own well-being or be a loser." This is President Bush's "ownership" message. Social responsibility says, "Be aware and take responsibility for the consequences of your self-interest." And, we should add that if one becomes aware of social consequences, then it is vital to care. If one becomes aware and doesn't care, it's a case of big boganism.

There is a caveat: people do become aware, do care, and do try to take responsibility for their consequences—at least some people some of the time. As true as this is, this happens in spite of the system, not because of it. The system and our culture are driven by the use of blinders put on us as we go about our personal lives. "Take responsibility for yourself and don't worry about the rest," it says. If some begin to get aware, care, and act, it's only because they were fortunate enough to either take off the blinders or have them removed through awakening experiences that broadened their perspective. And as much as this is happening today, it is not the system that is causing it.

Moreover, the economy motivates us to have all we can have and not worry about social and environmental consequences—that is, inequality and environmental collapse—on the assumption that more quantity creates more quality. Its point is that the individual pursuit of stuff will automatically advance the quality of life without having to take off the blinders. In other words, "You don't need to be socially aware, just produce and consume. The only consequence of more quantity is more quality."

This makes boganism an integral feature of capitalism and our freedom culture. Perhaps it is true that many corporations in the global economy are big bogans. They know that their self-interest is destroying the world. So they prefer to consciously pass the buck to the consumer, saying, "We wouldn't keep producing and supplying more of this stuff if people didn't buy it." Additionally, my local newspaper recently ran this headline: "Bush stands by rejection of limits on greenhouse gases" (Heilprin 2004, A1). This too may be a case of big boganism. If you think that the Administration is unaware of the consequences of a car-dependent, growth-driven economy, there's considerable evidence against you. Clearly, the Bush Administration believes that greenhouse gas limits will impede U.S. economic growth, cost jobs, and reduce profits. And this was admitted in the article. It points to two conclusions that reveal both big boganism and the two worst blinders: 1) you can grow forever on a finite planet, and 2) you have to have a profit-led economy to have jobs and anything else worth having.

Both are wrong. The first is becoming more and more obvious to more and more people around the world. And this is in part because little boganism can be educated out of existence. One thing we understand about our history is that people can learn. They have learned that slavery is no good. They've learned that smoking kills. And they are now learning that there are limits to growth. Awareness does happen. They are now just beginning to realize that more quantity doesn't necessarily equate to more quality, and that consequences matter.

The notion that you can run an economy without putting profits first is a tougher sell. And there are lots of big bogans who don't want that message broadcast. Big boganism is harder to deal with because the culprits know what they are doing; they simply don't care. "Stay the course," President Bush has said about the Iraq war. What about the consequences? Don't worry about them. The prevailing attitude in corporate circles, Washington, and their minions in the mainstream media is that firms should continue to pursue self-interest and profits-first decision making; the world should be as free from obstructions for this as possible; growth is unlimited if a miraculous technological fix can be found—and it will be; and government should do all it can to facilitate growth and the corporate agenda—which includes making people as insecure as possible by forcing them to compete and fend for themselves. This is in fact a bogan agenda—a big bogan agenda.

What's even bigger is the apparent commitment by the United States to succeed at being "the giant in the global village." This is being played out in Iraq, but it became fairly clear after 9/11. During the Cold War the notion that the United States needed to be an empire and a giant in that sense, resonated with Americans. And this was mostly a result of our perception that the Soviet Union had imperial designs—spreading communism—and was itself a giant. Additionally, what Marshall McLuhan coined in 1967 as the "global village" had yet to appear. But with the dismantling of the Soviet system after 1990, only one giant was left, communism was no longer a threat, and the world had been economically, technologically, and socially integrated into a global village. With the growth of interdependency among nations and peoples, today's global village doesn't need a giant. A giant in the global village—an empire in the midst of an interconnected village—simply doesn't work.

The profile of the United States is enormous in such a world. It's too easy to step on too many toes. The idea that a bigger stick will create stability doesn't fit. The world has outgrown the need for a giant or an empire. Giants can be taken down by terrorism. That should have been the message of 9/11 to the United States. A global village only makes sense if everyone in it agrees to be a villager on fairly equal terms. It's about equality of access to and control over resources. With the United States consuming five times its share of resources and creating that many times as much pollution, no wonder others see it as a giant and an empire. An excellent account of this is Mark Hertsgaard's *The Eagle's Shadow: Why America Fascinates and Infuriates the World* (2002). Hertsgaard states

> America faces a puzzling contradiction: We are by traditional measures the most powerful empire in all of human history, yet humanity has entered an era when no country, no matter how powerful, can adequately defend against the prevailing threats to health and security. We emerged as the last superpower at the very time when superpowers are becoming obsolete (204).

The current drift of the United States is to maintain its empire, be the giant, get a bigger stick, and if villagers don't like it and try to poke sticks at our toes, we call for regime change and preventive war, and step on them (Chomsky 2003). The big bogan is the giant itself. Pursue profits, expansion, be all you can be, have all you can have, insatiable growth, all the while disregarding the consequences by enforcing our way with imperial might. Is this likely to create biospheric sustainability? Is it likely to reduce inequality and create social justice? No. But there is a solution that takes us beyond boganism.

Awareness and Changed Minds Can Happen

One of the 20th century's most celebrated philosophers, Alfred North White-head (1861–1947) commented that "the major advances in civilization are the processes that all but wreck the societies in which they occur" (Whitehead 1979, 36). Although this calls our attention to what we are *doing* in the world, it is how we *are* in the world today that is the deeper cause. Going beyond boganism has a lot to do with becoming aware of consequences of how we are, not just how we behave. But Whitehead's remark illustrates something else. There has been since the beginning of civilizations—takerism—a tension between what humans are doing and their lack of awareness. There is a tendency for us to believe that what we experience in the world is the whole truth. And to save ourselves and the world, we need to clarify this.

Here's an example. The way we experience the world day to day is that the sun revolves around us. We watch it come up in the east and set in the west. And we use this experiential knowledge to grow our food. It works, and we say that *it is true* that the sun revolves around the earth. Then along comes Nicolaus Copernicus (1473–1543) at the beginning of capitalism and the scientific revolution, who tries to persuade humankind that the truth is just the opposite from what we experience—the earth revolves around the sun! Should we believe him? His argument is that there is something going on behind our backs that we are not aware of. Although we experience life one way, the truth of it is quite the opposite. Copernicus might as well have figured that people were wearing blinders. They weren't fully aware. The truth was different from their daily reality. His work was cut out for him, of course.

Karl Marx faced the same problem in trying to convince people in the mid-19th century that, contrary to the fact—the truth—of how they experienced it, capitalism is not a system of freedom but one of exploitation and injustice. It is clear from hindsight that people do tend to experience capitalism as freedom, and surely Milton Friedman and Ayn Rand would agree. History has vindicated Copernicus, but not Marx. Humans wouldn't have entered the space age and orbited the earth without Copernicus' truth. What about Marx? It's all about awareness. And there can be dual truths. On the one hand, we experience the sun revolving around us; on the other hand we know we revolve around it. In some sense, both are true. If we want to grow food, the Copernican truth is unnecessary. We know enough from experiential reality and truth to not plant our food on the north side of trees. If we want to go to the moon, we need Copernicus' truth. We may find that Marx was right—the system is one of injustice and exploitation. And it still can be one of (unequal) freedom. But when it comes to saving the world and calming our personal lives, it is perhaps time to become more aware of what's going on behind our backs. This is Copernicus' message to us. Without the broader awareness, Whitehead is right. And so is Ishmael, when he questioned why humans would go on destroying the world merely in order to live.

Awareness of the sources of your personal stress and their connection to both the economy and the culture in which you exist is the first step in what can be a healing process for you and the earth. The costs of not knowing about the root causes are great, and researchers are only beginning to assess them. For example Tim Kasser has written an excellent book, *The High Price of Materialism* (2002), in which he has tried to measure some of the costs to human well-being from the insatiable pursuit of have all you can have. Several studies conducted by Kasser, as well as other psychologists, demonstrate a strong inverse relationship between well-being and materialistic values. In one study with adolescents they found that teens who expressed a priority for being rich were 1.68 times as likely to have separation anxiety disorders. They were over twice as likely to be passive-aggressive and likewise to be schizotypal (difficulty having close relationships) if they prioritized being rich (15-17). With respect to insecurity, since we know it's built into the structure of our economy, Kasser comments

> My understanding of the connection among insecurity, a materialistic value orientation, and well-being is that sometimes people experience circumstances (nonnurturing parents, poverty, death, anxiety) that lead them to feel insecure. This causes unhappiness and dissatisfaction, as security needs must be satisfied for good psychological health. At the same time, insecurity also makes it likely that people will pursue materialistic aims, as both inner predispositions and external consumer culture suggest that resources can purchase security. Thus, materialistic values are both a symptom of an underlying insecurity and a coping strategy taken on in an attempt to alleviate problems and satisfy needs (42).

Although Kasser doesn't argue that insecurity is the essence of capitalism, the whip that makes us be more, his studies do suggest that insecurity points to the pursuit of having more. And to the extent that having more alleviates some of the insecurity, it becomes self-reproducing. Kasser closes his account with an aphorism from Muhammad, the Prophet of Islam: "Riches are not from abundance of worldly goods, but from a contented mind." Kasser adds, "Throughout this book I have presented scientific data to show the truth of Muhammad's statement: a life centered around making money and attaining renown is not meaningful" (97). That money doesn't buy happiness is cliché, of course. It helps buffer the hardship and the insecurity, however. But the point is to be aware of what's going on that is actually causing the unhappiness, the stress, and the insecurity in the first place. Kasser's studies suggest that the pursuit of more stuff is curing the symptom rather than going to the root of the problem.

Awareness of causes, however, will only lead to curing symptoms or to despair and resignation, unless this awareness is accompanied by a realistic vision of a solution. Vision of a way out is not enough. It has to be practicable: a solution that can be implemented, and hopefully, in our lifetime. Marx would not have spent his entire life trying to explain what he believed to be the truth of capitalism unless he was convinced that there was a real alternative to capitalism. And Daniel Quinn has made a convincing argument that nothing will happen without changed minds. Awareness of our roots in the productivist culture is part of what it takes to change minds, and a sense of optimism about a realizable alternative surely helps, as well.

Roadmaps Abound

The literature that speaks to solutions and alternative economies is vast. And this is encouraging in itself. For example, Quinn refers to the alternative as New Tribalism, suggesting that we need to go beyond taker civilization, understand what can be learned from our past and present leavers, and focus on smaller scale living (Quinn 1999). In some respects his is a call for a modern leaver culture that realizes the need to stop insatiable expansion and the control that it requires. Lester Brown calls the alternative an Eco-Economy, and referring to our current system as Plan A, Brown says it's time for Plan B (Brown 2001, 2003). David Korten in *The Post-Corporate World* (1999) calls it a Healthy Market Economy. Paul Hawken and Hunter and Amory Lovins refer to their alternative as Natural Capitalism (1999). Vandana Shiva, one of today's most recognized sustainable development theorists, talks about Earth Democracy (Shiva 2005). There's Duane Elgin's Voluntary Simplicity (1993). Jeremy Rifkin argues that although the American Dream, based on the goods life, is waning, it may be replaced by the European Dream, a third stage of human consciousness, that puts quality of life ahead of consumerism (Rifkin 2004). Of course these are merely a handful of well-documented reform alternatives. None would call them blueprints in the literal sense, but they are roadmaps to a sustainable future.

We have to be mindful of the odds weighing against us, too. As Jay Walljasper of *Utne* magazine cautions, "There is no set of easy answers, despite what the marketers of new convenience products would have us believe. But that doesn't mean we can't make real steps to take back our lives" (Walljasper 2003, 62). As we identify the causes of our stress and realize it is related to the mess the world is in, we also look around for others who share a similar feeling. They are there. And many are working on the roadmap of sustainability. We have to get creative, but solutions require knowing the causes of the problems and we're getting close. It's actually a case of problem-solving, rather than another link in the chain of insatiable improvements that have punctuated our taker past. In many respects what we face today is similar to the population-food scarcity problem faced by our Neolithic ancestors. We have to approach our future from the problem-solving angle, not the improvement angle.

The outlines being floated worldwide share a host of common principles. First, democracy. All agree that economic decision making at all levels needs to be *more* democratized. Much of today's inequality can be traced to the fact that workers, rural peasants, consumers, the unemployed, women, and many others do not have an *equal* say in the pivotal decisions that affect their lives. This is true within and between nations. In the United States, once a worker walks into the office or factory, democracy ends. Your labor belongs to the company. Corporate boardrooms need to be democratized with representation from communities where they operate, their workers, and consumers. But there's more. The IMF, the World Bank, and the WTO should be made accountable and responsible through democratic representation.

We've been groping our way to more democratic participation in the political sphere but not the economy. Even our governments are not fully democratized, as we know. Campaign finance reform is essential in the United States to stop corporate and wealthy elites' ability to buy their agendas from patron politicians. The media must be broadened to include dissenting and left voices. It's important to see democracy as an evolving process, a groping process in which there is no black and white. It is not the case that something is *either* democratic *or* it is not. We have to think in terms of broadening democratic decision making in all of the spheres of life where consequences of behavior have external effects on others. Democracy is a continuum from very limited on one end, to something very *full* on the other. But it's the fundamental means for creating a socially just world in which there is an end to sexism, patriarchy, racism, ethnic and religious domination, and nationalist oppression. Humans have only just begun the path to fully democratic and just living. But relative to what we've accomplished in the political sphere with constitutional and representative democracy, we still have a long way to go in the economy.

Marx's idea of socialism was, in fact, "the absence of alienated labor," and for the 200 hundred years that this idea has been bandied about it has eluded us. There are two reasons for this: 1) the blinders are still on, and 2) businesses don't want it to happen, as it would mean the end of their control over the work process. Yet, the goal is integral to a sustainable future, as it actually means democratic labor. When workers of all kinds and in all places have an equal say on the job, where there is "worker self-management," participatory and empowering work for all people, then we have achieved "economic democracy" equivalent to political democracy.

The goal is not as lofty as it might seem. There are plenty of examples of firms that are progressing in this direction, because they realize that workers find their jobs more meaningful and purposeful when they have a sense of ownership and participation. This makes them more productive, of course. It *can* put such businesses in a bind, as giving away some control can improve productivity and profits, but giving away too much can cost the company everything. On the other hand, Patagonia, Inc. and Interface, Inc. (the largest floor covering firm in the world), are only two such examples of successful democratizing firms that we should appreciate. The list of companies that have varying degrees of worker ownership, employee self-management, and other democratizing schemes is quite long. But democratic decision making in the economy is not a matter of U.S. public policy or commitment—yet.

The second principle is satiability. Virtually all of the roadmaps for a sustainable world call for more satiable living, less focus on materialism, and a conscious redirection away from have all you can have. They call for a shift towards quality of life, voluntary simplicity, and sufficiency in production, rather than maximization of profits and the multiplication of wants. These roadmaps reject the economic mainstream's assumption that human wants are unlimited—as if we were hapless victims of our fixed insatiable natures.

To be clear, we have to admit that because our being is unlimited—we do have the potential to always be more—our desires are unlimited. As true as this is, it doesn't mean that, therefore, there is nothing we can do to reel in these desires or that we have no choice but to be insatiable. We can choose to be as satiable as we want. Again, it's a matter of awareness. Insatiable wants are not an issue when the world is lightly populated and there's ample recuperative capacity. That was the case 200 years ago at the time of the Industrial Revolution. But as we become aware of what's happening today, it's much easier to say that it's time to be satiable in order to save ourselves and the planet.

Kenneth Boulding (1910–1993), a genius of 20th century economics, who joined the environmental movement in its infant years of the 1960s and coined the term, spaceship earth, once said, "The best possible innovation in our productive process is not a new technology but the conscious elimination of a want" (Boulding 1975). He was clearly in sync with Marshall Sahlins' idea that our leaver ancestors had "affluence without abundance" by limiting their wants to what was easily satisfied. On the other hand, the way of capitalism has been the "needless multiplication of wants," as Gandhi noted. He added that "a time is coming when those who are in the mad rush today of multiplying their wants, vainly thinking that they add to the real substance, real knowledge of the world, will retrace their steps and say, 'What have we done?'" (Gandhi 1990, 148). Since the majority of humanity has yet to ask, "What have we done?" capitalism's approach continues to be the relentless promotion of as many wants as possible, followed by the endless development of new technologies to satisfy them. And we end up on the productivist treadmill with lots of stress.

The idea that the goods life is actually contradictory to the good life, as we've seen, is as old as the ancient Greek philosophers—and then some. Thousands of years before Gandhi, Confucius (551–479 BC), the Buddha (Siddhartha Gotama, 563–483 BC), Jesus, Mohammad (570?–632 AD)—all as spiritual founders of world religions cautioned against materialism and preached simplicity in all things. In effect, the Neolithic Revolution that spawned takerism 10,000 years ago, created the original tension between insatiability and satiability. We've been living with and in that tension ever since. As soon as the idea of "more" took root in civilization, the world's religions, including one of the oldest—Hinduism—cautioned against it. With the embedded economies and the culture of security that held self-interest at bay, these religions and their spiritual and philosophical counterparts held sway. Capitalism and the culture of freedom overturned everything in the 16th century.

Today's call for a more satiable lifestyle is largely secular in character, because it is a reaction to the environmentally and socially destructive forces of the global market system. But it's being echoed by many religious leaders, like the Dalhi Lama and Thich Nhat Hanh in Buddhism, and Dr. James Dobson of Focus on the Family, the largest Christian conservative organization in the United States. In fact the United Methodist Church has produced a six-part video series, "Curing Affluenza," that features evangelical theologian, Tony Campolo (de Graaf, Wann, and Naylor 2001, 180).

The principle of satiability is a logical extension of the awareness that it's capitalism's fixation on ever more stuff that's destroying the planet. But none of this speaks to the deeper issue of being all you can be. Most roadmaps detour when they encounter insatiable self-development. They don't want to go there. That's why what you are reading here is radical. The principle of satiability that is pivotal to the sustainability literature is surely valid as far as it goes.

The insatiable appetite for more material things is fundamental to capitalism, of course. Our deeper challenge is to understand where the obsession with more consumer goods actually originated. The answer? It evolved as we've seen from the obsession with being more, improving more, and developing more. Additionally, the obsession with always being more is no more genetic than that of having more. Neither one have a long history.

The third principle common to the roadmaps of sustainability is that of smaller scale. The scale of production, consumption, urban and suburban living, and all of the associated congestion of too many people with too much stuff, has been accelerating since the Industrial Revolution. The roadmaps argue that we need to scale back our lives and our economic activity to something more manageable—to a more human scale. E. F. Schumacher (1911–1977), another of the many pioneering economists of the 1960s environmental movement, called our attention to the dehumanizing effects of massive, larger-than-life scale in the early 1970s. His book, *Small Is Beautiful: Economics as if People Mattered* (1973) is a classic. Chapter Four, "Buddhist Economics," was first published in *Resurgence* magazine in its premier issue in 1968.

The editors declared, "We envision a Fourth World where government and economics are under genuine human control because the size of such units are small, sensible, and human scale, where there is a maximum of decentralized decision making, and where the pace of change is regulated not by the appetites of an overmighty minority for profit and power, but by the day-to-day needs of small-scale human communities and the psychic capacities of their members to adapt" (McClaughry 1989, *x*). This continues to be the message of the roadmaps today. Quinn's notion of New Tribalism speaks to this, as well. The scale of human economic and social activity—that of leavers both then and now—was small, personal, and intimate. We can't go back, but we can surely learn that what in part made leaverism so sustainable for so long was its small scale.

How do we scale down and decentralize? The "think globally; act locally" movement is an important step. There is clearly a lot of support for more decentralized living, the shift to local level autonomy in politics, and community control over resources. The growing movement by local communities to stop the growth of "big box" stores, like Super Wal-Marts and Home Depot, is one such case. Many who are not particularly leftwing or environmental are still behind the movements to make both government and business accountable to people at the local level. And there's growing awareness that "community"—a sense of belonging to people and place—is virtually impossible in the dehumanized scale that surrounds us.

Another development is that of bioregionalism. Bioregions are biological regions determined by the types of ecosystems within them. They have geographic boundaries rather than human or politically-determined borders. These regions differ by the kinds of life that they support and the kinds of plants and animals that are native to them. The United Sates has bioregions but our production, consumption, towns, and cities are not organized with that in mind. With bioregionalism humans live *with* natural systems rather than trying to force nature to adapt to our wishes. Bioregionally, it makes no sense to grow cotton in the Phoenix, Arizona valley when the only source of water is the Central Arizona Project's pipeline diverting it from the Colorado River over 200 hundred miles away.

Bioregionalism puts a premium on smaller scale by suggesting that humans should live within their means dictated by the biological environments around them. Bioregionalism dovetails with both permaculture/sustainable agriculture techniques relying on what Schumacher called appropriate technologies—those that are sized for human scale—and with strategies for local, food self-sufficiency and local production of basic goods and services. It is an approach that also offers viable means for sustainable development in the poorest parts of our world. Bioregionalism as a movement is about forty years old, but as a way to survive sustainably with human scale it is our oldest source of knowledge about how to live. "The essence of bioregionalism is what we can best remember and piece together of the oldest earth traditions and wisdom, tracing back to the beginnings of humanity." It has been the "reality and common sense for native people living close to the land for thousands of years and remains so for human beings today" (Permaculture Activist 2005).

In effect bioregionalism argues that we need to organize our basic material needs, and especially food production, to what we can sustainably produce and consume in our local regions. What about all those bananas that Iowans eat? You can't grow them in Iowa, so they have to be imported. You can sustainably and organically grow a wide variety of other food crops in Iowa. Importing bananas is not living bioregionally. It doesn't mean that Iowans must totally give them up. But their price today doesn't accurately reflect their environmental and social cost of production and it should. Bioregionalism suggests that those who live in Costa Rica should eat lots of bananas and grow other basic foods that are also native to their region. There will clearly be trade between regions and nations in a future sustainable economy, but the trade needs to be subordinated to what works bioregionally.

The scaling down of our production and lifestyles, as bioregionalism maintains, implies a shift to local self-sufficiency. This is even more important as a development strategy for places like Africa. We have to recall that everywhere in the world, for most of our human history, humans were self-sufficient. Trade existed then, and it will in the future, but to move forward to smaller scale living, we need to refocus on self-sufficiency, starting with agriculture. Many development theorists, like Vandana Shiva, have embraced this. Activists in the Southern Hemisphere, like 2004 Nobel Peace Prize recipient, Kenyan professor, Wangari Maathai, have embraced it.

The UN's Food and Agriculture Organization announced in late 2004 that for the first time in nine years, the number of malnourished people in the world has increased. With 80 percent of the world's hungry in rural areas and over half of them subsistence farmers, the bioregional strategy fits perfectly. Milla McLachlan, the nutrition advisor for the World Bank stated that Brazil's Zero Hunger Program is an excellent model for bioregional development that addresses both hunger and food security. Rather than handing out food Brazil's program offers free school lunches but the food provided comes from local small and medium sized farmers, who then earn income that helps sustain their living. This is rural development that not only maintains the small farmer but addresses hunger as well. Funds invested in rural development to reduce hunger are estimated to return as much as 20 times their cost in benefits at the local level (Becker 2004, 2). Smaller scale living and basic self-sufficiency go hand-in-hand. Trade and the international division of labor in production and agriculture, instead of determining where we live, how we live, and what we produce, need to take a backseat to more democratic, satiable, and decentralized living.

The point for our roadmaps is not that North Americans have to give up bananas. It's that we want to live less stressful lives, have a stronger feeling of community, and feel that our local communities are under our decentralized, democratic control rather than feeling like we are at the mercy of the market or Wal-Mart. Eating fewer bananas is perhaps a small price to pay for what we gain by going bioregional.

Such a strategy is much closer to an "ownership society" than President Bush would have us believe. It's largely impossible to have a sense of belonging, a feeling of community, and a participatory lifestyle when the only thing we share with our neighbors is the street or the housing complex we inhabit and the fact that we are all in a competitive struggle of "antagonistic cooperation." When each is merely on his or her own in the struggle to get ahead, consumerism is the only antidote. We find ourselves competing to see whose house is biggest. On the other hand, bioregionalism offers us a way to appreciate "small is beautiful." When neighbors have more in common than residences, when their community members are working together to meet each other's needs, the sense for taking care of each other and assuring one another's security takes on new meaning and fulfillment. Bioregionalism is not the cure-all by itself, but it contributes to more democracy and more satiable living by calling our attention to quality of life rather than quantity.

A Cultural Revolution with Economic Reforms

Reform or revolution? What's it going to take? Both. But it's less complicated than you might think. Figure 2.1 helps clarify this. The inside circle of the economy can be transformed with "reforms," while the outside circle of our culture requires "revolution." But the revolution can be one not of violence and conflict, but of changed minds, as Quinn suggests. With a different set of values and a new understanding of our human place in the community of life, a revolution will have occurred. It's not a scary event or process.

The roadmaps for sustainability offer three basic principles, but we haven't gotten to the specifics. What most worries people about social change is how realistic it is and whether or not it is too overwhelming, too huge, to take seriously. Usually it is the economy that's at issue. Fortunately, to the save the world and yourself, the economy can be transformed with a package of radical reforms. The reforms themselves are not radical, and in fact, most have been implemented in a number of countries quite successfully. What makes them radical is when they are implemented on a *comprehensive* basis rather than piecemeal or *ad hoc*. For example, it doesn't do much good to raise the minimum wage in the United States if it only causes businesses to outsource jobs or reduce production. Likewise, tougher environmental legislation and enforcement is less effective when firms can circumvent or subvert it by closing down operations and investing in real estate or shift production overseas where there are lower compliance costs.

In figure 4.2 we have a triangle.

Figure 4.2. Profits Before People

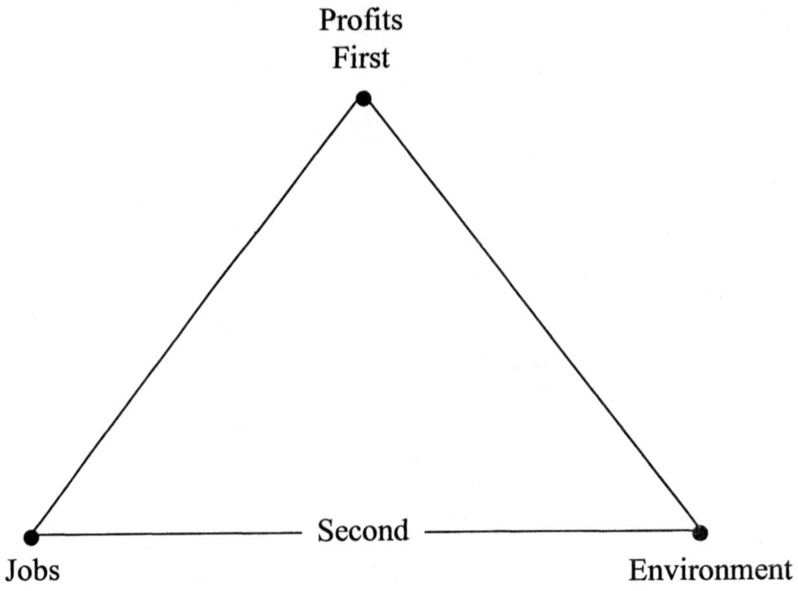

Profits
First

Jobs   Environment

Profits are at the apex, as they are in capitalism. Underneath, and subordinate, are jobs on the one hand and the environment on the other. The system and corporate spokespeople, at least since the 1960s, have asked their workers and consumers to choose between jobs or protection/preservation of the environment. Corporate ideologues tell us that if we want to have jobs, then we can't afford viable environmental legislation. The labor movement has spoken on behalf of workers, saying that jobs have to come first. What good is clean air if one is unemployed and on the streets? While, on the other hand, if environmentalists demand stronger laws forcing corporations to clean up their act, businesses tell us that it will cost jobs. This has pitted the labor movement against the environmental movement for forty years. The corporate view is that we can't have both. So let the people choose. This is precisely what President Bush stated in refusing to sign off on the Kyoto Protocol in 2004. His justification was that to do so would cost jobs. "President Bush strongly opposes any treaty or policy that would cause the loss of a single American job, let alone the nearly 5 million jobs Kyoto would have cost," stated James Connaughton, Bush's Chair of the White House Council on Environmental Quality (Heilprin 2004, A1).

There is a myth that must be dispelled: we can't have both. Yes, we can. Corporations and their ideologues don't say that we must make these hard choices because profits have to come first. They don't directly mention the top priority given to maximizing profits. If we pin them down, they might mention profits, but are then quick to reply that without profits the entire system would collapse. There's truth to this, of course. In a profit-motivated system, if firms can't make the profits they expect, then they don't invest, we don't get jobs, and a crisis results. So most of time, we are stuck with *either* profits and jobs *or* profits and a cleaner environment. Additionally, it should be clear that we can substitute a whole range of needs and issues for jobs and the environment.

There's health insurance, higher pay, worker participation, better working conditions, a shorter work week, more opportunities for women and people of color, and so on. The bottom line is that working people are placed, unknowingly, into an unnecessary tradeoff without being told the whole truth. If business is going to allow all three needs of the pyramid to be met, it is only so on the basis of substantial economic growth—more for everybody. But more economic growth is not sustainable. In fact, the economic growth that has occurred since the 2001 recession has seen a decrease in new jobs in the United States and deterioration in environmental quality and enforcement. President Bush's 2006 budget request actually cuts the EPA budget.

To have what the people want and need, it is the case that profits must be subordinated to these broader social needs. And the set of economic reforms we subsequently offer will do this. The triangle needs to be inverted, in other words, so that it looks like Figure 4.3.

Figure 4.3. People Before Profits

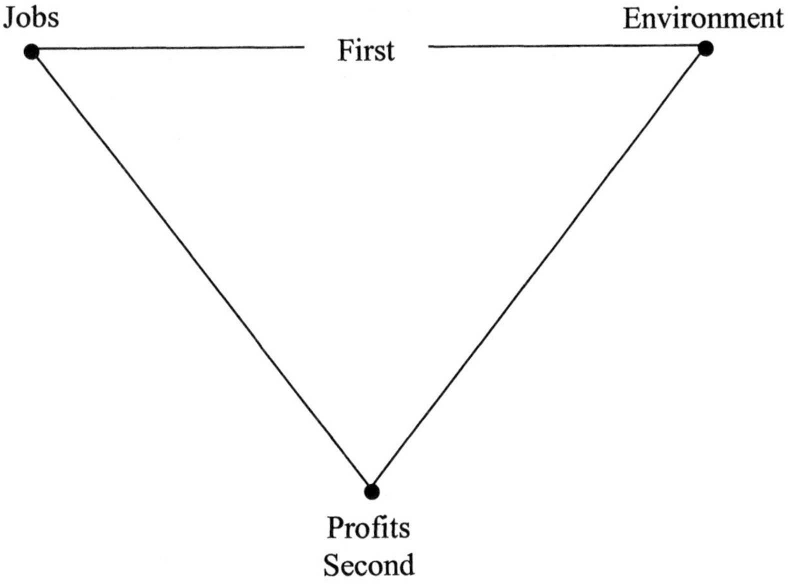

The idea of putting people before profits has consistently terrified the corporate class for two centuries. Their defenders will say that it won't work, and we will refute this. The alternative notion of reconciling people and profits, what all politicians love to spout, can happen but only under very qualified circumstances. As we've said, economic growth is held out as the panacea. Of course, growth occurs only if it is profitable for firms to invest in the first place. Doing so usually comes at the expense of other people, like in the third world, or the environment (frequently in the third world as well). Unprecedented U.S. economic growth after World War II did help reconcile profits and people—people in the United States, that is, and mostly white males in the United States—but only because of cheap oil and other resources, and ample new market and investment opportunities overseas. By denying, for example, the Middle East control over its own oil, U.S. growth brought working people and business together after the class conflict of the 1930s. Businesses conceded unionization to American workers after the War, bringing higher wages and better working conditions, but only because oil was exploitatively cheap. Cheap energy compensated profits that otherwise would have suffered from higher wage costs.

Today we face a new set of conditions in which growth is not a solution. We have to choose between people and profits. Thus the pyramid has to be flipped. What does this imply? It's not as bad as corporations and politicians suggest. The reforms are just that—reforms. They will subordinate profit making to our more pressing human needs, all of which will increase the quality of life for the majority, reduce your stress and anxiety, and assure decent material security with more equality. This does not spell the end of business or the end of profits. It's simply a strategy to shift priorities from stockholders to workers and citizens. It's about democratizing the corporate boardroom. There will be redistribution of wealth and decision-making power. The elites will be on the losing end, of course.

But businesses have made concessions to the people in the past, and they can be pressed to do so again. Popular, mass-based, public pressure brought about the Social Security Act in 1935. Businesses did not endorse it and tried to oppose and defeat it. They lost but didn't throw in the towel. They stayed in the game. They again lost battles after World War II. And in the late 1960s and early 1970s, they were pressured to accept Medicaid, Medicare, the Equal Employment Opportunity Act, the Occupational Safety and Health Act, the Civil Rights Act, and the Clean Air and Water Act. They tried to defeat all of this legislation and failed. But they conceded defeat and continued to stay in the game, as they had done in the 1930s. The challenge we face today is no different. With enough public pressure for reforms that are based on sound reasoning and our common need to save the planet, they will concede.

There are examples, too, of where the shift to a sustainable and just global economy will actually enhance profitability. The Lovins and Paul Hawken's *Natural Capitalism*, along with Rifkin's *The Hydrogen Economy* detail the many businesses that are currently discovering that doing the right thing for the environment and the people—social and environmental responsibility—stimulates profits. Some of these cases are niche market situations. Others are not, for example, the case of Interface, Inc. Interface has to compete in a global market but has found that doing the right thing has actually helped. The point is that there are already precedents and role models for businesses' ability to put people before profits. Yvon Chouinard, founder and owner of Patagonia, Inc. states

> As an alpinist who set out to make gear for my friends and never thought of myself as a 'businessman' until long after I became one, I've wrestled the demons of corporate responsibility for some time. Who are the businesses really responsible to? Their shareholders? Their customers? Their employees? None of the above, I have finally come to believe. Fundamentally, businesses are responsible to their resource base. Without a healthy planet there are no shareholders, no customers, no employees. As the conservationist David Brower liked to say, 'There is no business to be done on a dead planet.' (Chouinard 2004, 37).

Of course, at the same time that Yvon Chouinard, as a CEO, is embracing an ethic of environmental justice, there is Wal-Mart Corporation, the world's biggest retailer, who is actively working to undermine such values. When the Texas Wal-Mart meat cutters voted to join the United Food and Commercial Workers union a few years ago, Wal-Mart management closed all of the meat cutting departments in the state. In 2004, the Quebec Wal-Mart employees voted to unionize. Again, Wal-Mart responded by closing the store in February 2005. Every roadmap's principle of democracy involves aggressive defense of workers' rights to have a union. And of the essential reforms that must be implemented in order to invert the pyramid of profits-first is the fundamental one of fostering worker democracy through democratic and participatory unions.

The economic reforms that must be implemented speak to the principles of democracy, satiability, and smaller scale. The pyramid can be overturned by their implementation. Along with public policy at the federal level to foster unionization and employee organizing, there needs to be an Economic Bill of Rights. This would enforce the tenets of the UN Declaration of Human Rights, Article 25, which says that "Everyone has the right to a standard of living adequate for the health and well-being of herself and of her family, including food, clothing, housing, and medical care and necessary social services, and the right to security in the event of unemployment, sickness, disability, widowhood, old age, or other lack of livelihood in circumstances beyond her control" (Korten 1999, 168). Obviously, this implies a shift from earned security to assured security.

Over two decades ago a group of economists presented an exemplary Bill that included 24 rights. Among these are the right to a decent job, comparable pay and equal employment opportunity, a shorter standard work week and flexible hours, flexible price controls, promotion of community enterprises, workers' right to know and decide, democratizing investment decisions, democratizing foreign trade, renewable energy commitment, sustainable agriculture, public childcare, a national health policy, and equitable taxation (Bowles, Gordon, and Weisskopf 1984, 270).

The specifics of such a Bill are less important than the public commitment to the concept itself. An Environmental Bill of Rights is also needed, as the former speaks to social justice, while the Environmental Bill would focus on environmental justice. The issues are as ideological and controversial today as they were a hundred years ago. Capitalism has accepted a Bill of Rights in the political sphere but never in the economic sphere.

The extension of rights to the economy is the most essential reform we can implement, as it would be the pivotal democratizing agent. The reforms needed to supplement an Economic and Environmental Bill of Rights would have to include an increase in the minimum wage to at least $10 an hour; national health insurance and a public health delivery system; restoration of the corporate income tax to 1950s levels; a "green tax" that taxed environmentally harmful products; subsidies for renewable energy development; an industrial policy that brought business together with the government to share information, pricing, and investment decisions—based on cooperation rather than competition; a national jobs program that offered anyone willing to work a job at a livable wage with a democratic say on the job; a mass transit development project; an urban redevelopment program that included a jobs component; and a public chartering system for corporations, forcing them to democratize their boardrooms and serve the public interest—one of David Korten's ideas. Still, this is only a partial list.

Internationally, the corporate players and nations of the global economy need to begin the shift from a competitive system to a cooperative one. One means to this end is to democratize the financial and development organizations of the UN, World Bank, IMF, and WTO. Representation in these agencies, excluding the UN, is not democratic as they serve now as vehicles of corporate expansion and control. The peoples of the poorest regions of the world are underrepresented. But this can change.

These reforms, all of which would costs profits, are not extraordinary. Many of the European nations have such legislation and the evidence to show that these reforms work. The Social Democratic tradition in Europe has a rich history of industrial planning, viable social safety nets, worker participation, nation-wide collective bargaining, green taxes, and national health care. One is often tempted to argue, as our corporate ideologues do, that a system of high taxes, substantial government intervention for regulation and public ownership, and social welfare spending can't work. The Europeans have been demonstrating otherwise for decades. That's been another well-kept secret. Jeremy Rifkin's recent book, *The European Dream: How Europe's Vision of the Future is Quietly Eclipsing the American Dream* (2004), not only tries to expose the successes of the European model of capitalism—one that is less individualistic, more cooperative and collective—but argues that the U.S. dream is antiquated. The American Dream, once that of the entire capitalist world, suggests that pursuit of self-interest maximizes the general interest, while it simultaneously equates the goods life with the good life.

The new European dream is quite the opposite. It is based on the principle that pursuit of the general interest is what actually maximizes self-interest. This is so, because when humans shift their focus from quantity of stuff to quality of life, many of the attributes of quality are realized by working together in a more collective, democratic, and cooperative fashion. In other words, once people begin to hunger for social meaning and purpose and desire greater quality of relationships with others, and more security and less stress, they notice a strange inversion of Adam Smith's invisible hand: putting the general interest first maximizes self-interest. Working together in the most just, fair, and democratic manner works. Cooperation works better than competition when what you want out of life is more meaning, fulfillment, more satisfying relations with your co-workers, family, community, and less anxiety.

Businesses need to work together, to get beyond the control asserted by Wall Street and the greed of their shareholders. They need to sit down both within industries and between them, both at the domestic and international levels, and collectively and democratically collaborate on playing their part in a sustainable economy of the future. Rifkin suggests that such a forum is now opening in Europe: the European Union itself. Any notion of businesses "working together" as been anathema to the American political and economic scene since the 1890s. When the Roosevelt Administration proposed the National Industrial Recovery Act of 1933, it was declared unconstitutional by 1935. Why? Restraint of trade and collusion. Such behavior on the part of business would violate consumer sovereignty, according to conventional economic wisdom. Americans have feared business collusion, while businesses have feared worker collusion—that is, unions. If there is no democratization of corporate decision making, and competition rules the market, then of course, a lack of competition will redistribute power in the wrong direction. But if all the avenues are opened up to public and worker democracy, so that all affected parties have an equal say, then what happens? Collusion—that is, getting together to lord it over others—turns into cooperation for the general interest. That's where we need to go, and perhaps the European Union will become a role model for this.

Cooperation and collective production can work as long as there is democratic decision making. Planning can work as long as it is democratically done—which it never was in the former Soviet economic model. Productivity has been shown to increase—as long as there is democratic decision making. Incentives other than financial have been shown to work—as long as there is democratic and participatory input.

And then there's the current flourishing of "non-profits" and "not-for-profits." They are the fastest growing business organization today. Their track record for efficiency is excellent. Even the 20th century's management guru and acclaimed scholar, Peter Drucker, once told *Forbes* magazine that the Salvation Army (one of 60,000 U.S. charitable organizations) was one of the best managed businesses in the United States. It's very efficient, highly productive, and delivers the most service for the least cost of about any of the Fortune 500 firms. Drucker stated that it is "by far the most effective organization in the U.S. No one even comes close to it in respect to clarity of mission, ability to innovate, measurable results, dedication and putting money to maximum use" (Lenzner and Ebeling 1997, 1). Yet it's a nonprofit (Drucker 1992). There are more than eight million workers in the nonprofit sector of the U.S. economy, as well as an additional 80 million volunteers. The sector is viable and flourishing, based on cooperation rather than competition, and often promotes democratic decision making as a vehicle to enhance performance and employee buy-in and enthusiasm.

Profits aren't going to go away. Neither are management, trade, marketing, accounting, corporations, the IMF and WTO, prices, and money. What needs to happen, and can happen, is that these mechanisms of capitalism have to be reshaped and redirected to serve new goals—sustainability and social justice, sufficiency and simplicity, tranquility and equality. The radical reforms will do this—on one condition. A cultural revolution must take place—changed minds. If we can make this happen, the rest will be easy.

Cultural Revolution and Paradigm Shift

The kind of revolution we are talking about is comparable to both the Industrial Revolution and the Agricultural Revolution, not the Bolshevik Revolution—a "political" revolution only. This transformation in our consciousness should also be viewed as a paradigm shift, as the dominant paradigm and culture today says that the purpose of a human life is to insatiably develop it and everything good around it. If you are beginning to question the imperative of insatiable development and self-actualization, if you are starting to rethink the necessity to always be more tomorrow than you are today, then you are already in the new paradigm. That's not too difficult. Your mind has changed. What about everyone else though? And what about getting the radical reforms implemented? That's harder.

One of the prospective publishers of this book expressed concern that since its theme is that we need to change how we view ourselves and get passed our modern fixation on insatiable self- and social-development, it would be a "politically deeply pessimistic" message. No one would want to read or hear it, because "it is not realistic to see personal or political action that could overturn such deeply rooted orientations." Clearly, if productivism is working for you, and you're not overly stressed, and being all you can be is thrilling, and you fail to see the world as self-destructive, then the message is perhaps lost on you. But if you are concerned about the world and your own fulfillment, then a paradigm shift—changing your mind—is not pessimistic but often liberating. And talking to those in your midst who might also feel as you is not so frustrating.

Daniel Quinn commented that although changing minds sounds like an endless task, it's not. He noted that about one million people have read *Ishmael*, and on the assumption that it changed their minds, if the following year each one changed the mind of one other person, the second year we'd have two million converts. If in subsequent years each person changed the mind of only one other individual, it would only take about a dozen years to have the whole world's six billion people thinking the new paradigm. Of course, for the first million, they would have to change a mind each year for twelve years to make the math work.

But by doubling the number of new thinkers each year, the job can be done in your lifetime!

The Agricultural Revolution took place over several thousand years, and some would say twice that. The Industrial Revolution took about two centuries. These were cultural revolutions that changed the way people thought about themselves and their relationship to the earth. The cultural revolution that we are suggesting is similar but may proceed much faster. This is in part due to the fact that it is a problem-solving revolution, in which humans are finding it easier and easier to observe the problem of environmental destruction first-hand. Communication is rapid and education is better than ever. Changing minds can go quickly once people feel the need to do so.

The economic reforms can go quickly once there is a critical mass of changed minds. History tells us that to usher in a new world based upon satiability and sustainability, it will take more than a 51 percent majority. Corporations have to come onboard; the wealthy elites of the world have to make some concessions and submit to public pressure. I suspect that it will take an 80 percent majority to make this happen. And the logical sequence of events is that progressive movements all over the world will continue as they are now doing to build coalitions and networks that align their causes, campaigns, and projects. The World Social Forum will get bigger. New alliances will continuously form, as leaders organize and reach out. Women; labor; environmental; human rights; anti-sweatshop; corporate accountability; voluntary simplicity; nationalist, ethnic, and religious autonomy; consumer; socialist; sustainable development; all of these movements, though separable with respect to campaigns have the potential to come together. World systems theorist, Immanuel Wallerstein, comments that the World Social Forum "is the most important social movement now on the face of the earth and the only one that has a chance of playing a really significant role. It has blossomed very fast" (Wallerstein 2004, 46). It is a movement of movements, in part because it has "no hierarchical center, is tolerant of all the varieties within it, and yet stands for something" (46). This may perhaps galvanize the 80 percent majority. Why would they coalesce? Because they share a common adversary—a culture and economy driven by the idea that more is better. They share a common goal and dream—a world based on quality of life, where equality, democracy, and justice rule over self-interested greed and competition. Jeremy Rifkin states that "In a sustainable civilization, based on quality of life rather than unlimited individual accumulation of wealth, the very material basis of modern progress would be a thing of the past. A sustainable, steady-state economy is truly the end of history defined by unlimited material progress" (Rifkin 2004, 7-8). If this should occur, it would be a paradigm shift comparable to the Industrial and Agricultural Revolutions.

Beyond Improvement for Its Own Sake

When you consider what it would take to leave your stress behind and live in a less driven system, something like a "steady-state economy," as Rifkin mentions, there are a few obvious questions. We've grown accustomed to continuous improvement of everything. Reflective people always ask about how we could ever live without more improvement of health care and disease research to fight AIDS and cancer, for example. Shouldn't we always try to improve? And what about being more? Shouldn't we at least be trying to be more virtuous and be better people?

With respect to improvements that reduce suffering, there is every reason to believe that we can and will continue to examine and fund research that reduces needless suffering. But we can, as a matter of global policy and consensus brought about through international forums, prioritize the list of needed research and improvements. We can choose democratically and fairly the areas that we need to fund to find cures and techniques that will save lives and reduce suffering. The focus of improvement needs to shift to that of alleviating suffering rather than that of improvement for its own sake.

And suffering is a complicated issue, as well. There are forms of suffering that will never be eliminated—some due to accidents, some that are existential, like the grief of losing a loved one. We can try to reduce the accidents by making the world a safer and more secure place. We can reduce the grief from loss by making the world a more just place with fewer violent conflicts and wars. We can reduce the loss of life and suffering that stems from auto congestion and smoking-related cancers by creating a less car-dependent world where people have more fulfilling lives that require fewer addictions to cope and be happy.

The key issue with improvement-to-reduce-suffering is this: suffering can be dignified or not. Humans can suffer with dignity or by lack of it. What improvement should be about is the effort to reduce and eliminate all those forms of suffering that result from lives that lack dignity. The suffering of malnourishment and poverty; the suffering of women from male domination and patriarchy;

the suffering from needless wars and domestic violence; the suffering of unemployment hardship; the suffering from racism and all other forms of domination, injustice, and oppression—these are suffering due to a lack of dignity. But the grief and suffering from accidental death and tragedies that can't be avoided, that are no one's fault, can be at least dignified. It can be suffering that is not demeaning or degrading to either the victims or their survivors. Our leaver ancestors surely had their share of suffering and hardship, but because their lives were about taking care of each other rather than the pursuit of self-interest, they didn't lack dignity. There wasn't humiliation.

Hardship? Isn't the insatiable improver economy about reducing "hardship?" The ideologues say so. But is it working? Not when there is more poverty than nine years ago, and many of us are continually under the stress to always be more. Not when Americans, with one of the highest standards of living in the world, actually work longer hours today than 50 years ago. The modern capitalist way to deal with hardship is to try to eliminate it through technological progress. The leaver way of our ancestors was to make sense out of it. The unnecessary hardship endured by the poor and dispossessed of the world is one that we can eliminate, of course. But the notion that any type of hardship, even in a socially just world, should be unthinkingly attacked is problematic. How much stuff is enough in this respect? As long as humans have an economy and culture that says that any hardship should be automatically taken to task puts us back in the unsustainable path of improvement for its own sake.

Why Be More?

A new culture of sustainability and satiability wouldn't require us to be more. It would accept the idea that unused human potential is *not* waste. So you want to be more without having more? You want to be more virtuous and be a better person? That's fine. Go for it, but don't expect everyone to do likewise, and don't expect to live in a culture that measures you by these kinds of accomplishments or to live in an economy that drives you to this. It's your choice, and as long as trying to be more or improve your skills doesn't result in consequences that contradict the principles of sustainability and justice, it is all right.

For example, the life story of John Wesley Powell is interesting because he was remarkably ambitious but wasn't big on improvement. As the first Anglo explorer to run the entire length of the uncharted Colorado River through the Grand Canyon and beyond in 1869, and doing this sight-unseen and with a one-arm disability from the Civil War, Powell displayed tremendous personal, and in many respects, selfish ambition and initiative. He funded this venture entirely out of his own pocket. He clearly had a mission with goals to accomplish and achieve—he was driven. And while he did succeed on the Colorado River, it is apparent from his biography that he was not motivated by self-development, nor by the desire for social and economic development. He, in fact, went back to Washington, D.C. and argued that the American West should not be developed. He lost. The driven-takers of the East insisted on insatiable improvement and development.

But his life story does testify to the idea that we can be ambitious without being insatiable self-developers. Additionally, there is a real difference between facing and enjoying personal challenges on the one hand, and being a productivist—being all you can be. A good physical or intellectual challenge that one finds gratifying isn't the same as bowing to the imperative of always having to be more. Consequently, the purpose of our new cultural paradigm is to motivate the economy without compulsion to be more and without need to have more.

What would motivate us then? Responsibility. An economy of sufficiency would reward people for being responsible, for not being bogans, in other words. The preamble of the Earth Charter states this, as well. "To realize these aspirations, we must decide to live with a sense of universal responsibility, identifying ourselves with the whole Earth community as well as our local communities. Everyone shares responsibility for the present and future well-being of the human family and the larger living world" (Earth Charter 2005). Today, responsibility is clearly a trait we recognize and appreciate, but it's not what we reward. We reward productivism—being more. In an economy not driven by improvement, "pulling your weight," "being there" for your coworkers and colleagues, and "shouldering your share of the responsibility," and being dependable and reliable would matter the most. And this would be an economy, obviously, that is about taking care of each other rather than getting ahead. It would put a premium on collective and cooperative production rather than competitive production.

If you want to be more and self-develop, that's your business but for those of us who don't, this would be a culture that wouldn't penalize us or consider us "losers" simply because we're not productivists like you. You can be more, but you don't have to be, and no one will think less of you as long as you are socially and individually responsible. Such a principle of morality and behavior is far more consistent with the religious teachings of the past, and far more what Aristotle had in mind for the path of virtue and happiness.

Quinn has pointed out that humans and many of their religions today have a peculiar notion that a better world is possible—but only if people were better. But we often feel, he argues, that we are flawed beings who will never get it right and must therefore seek salvation. He's right about something: we don't need to be better people to make it work. None of the reforms or culture change requires us to be better than we are. We simply have to shift the motivating incentives from our greedy, self-interested side to our collective and cooperative side. Humans, as we know, are not one-dimensional beings with a fixed nature. We got off on the wrong path, as Quinn says, about 10,000 years ago—we took the taker road and ended up here as driven-takers. We have created staggering amounts of wealth by using the selfish side of our being. And we use the caring and sharing side today, too. It's still there. The difference is that we drive the economy with self-interest and reserve our sharing side for our private lives. The alternative is to use the sharing and caring side to run the economy and reserve the selfish side for private pursuits. We aren't flawed, nor do we need to be better people. We simply need to tweak our motivations a bit and put them in a different cultural context.

If Being More Isn't a Priority, What Is?

A culture of sustainability and an economy of sufficiency would put responsibility, problem-solving, maintenance, security, justice/democracy, and equality first. This path would reroute humankind from driven-takerism to what might be called "dignified survival." Our leaver ancestors were satiable survivors, while our current culture is one of insatiable improvers. To be sustainable and accept a more subordinate role in the community of life, we need a new foundation based more on maintenance than development and more about survival-with-dignity than improvement. Quality of relationships would replace the accumulation of stuff. A feeling of belonging and of being needed would substitute for trophy hunting. We have to begin thinking in terms of "equal simplicity" and "diverse equality" as principles of sustainability. Certainly, incomes will not be completely equal. Some will be rewarded by their coworkers, some will have more skills and qualifications, some will have more responsibility, and some will work more than others. The principle that each should be able to spend their incomes in order to maximize satisfaction of their particular tastes and preferences is valid. And cultural diversity, religious diversity, and ethnic diversity will and must be appreciated. Why not? None of these concerns or aspirations is inconsistent with the principles of sustainability.

Development and improvement, both of the self and the social, are not bad. But they aren't necessary either. We can run the economy without them as the driving force. The purpose is to create the social conditions and institutions that make living justly, simply, and sustainably not only possible but easy.

You can reduce your stress by understanding it. You may not be able to eliminate it in this lifetime. Joining any of the many progressive movements in your town, in your region or nation, or at your workplace, and participating with others that share your dreams of a safer and more just world is a powerful antidote to resignation and despair, as you already know. We're not bogans, and we don't have to be more to make it work. Being responsible and thinking about consequences, changing a mind or two—you might replace stress with meaning and purpose. The endless pursuit of personal freedom and self-actualization is insatiable. On the other hand, security and taking care of each other, the guiding principles of leaver peoples is satiable. These are norms that have been proven to work and can be resurrected for our future. It's merely a different awareness, and one that doesn't require all that much from us. But we have to want it.

The Collective Self-Help To-Do List

It would be nice in our efforts to just "be"—knowing that being is enough—if we didn't have to address a to-do list. Of course, Mooch's approach is good: "This should be intereshting." But this to-do list is more about being responsible than being all we can be. There are four pressing challenges for all of us as citizens of the global village: 1) turn globalization of capitalism from a corporate-led, competitive struggle to a people-led cooperative enterprise, 2) dismantle the U.S. Empire, 3) end patriarchy, and 4) reduce human population.

The first agenda item is about democratizing the global economy. Some call it globalization from the bottom up, since the issue is not that life today is global, but that it is hierarchically global. Others have called it deglobalization to emphasize the need to decentralize and scale down our interdependent world, so that democratic decision making can work more effectively. The second task on our agenda is to first make it clear to all, particularly in the United States, that it is an Empire. As Indian novelist and activist, Arundhati Roy has stated

> Until quite recently, it was sometimes difficult for people to see themselves as victims of Empire. But now, local struggles have begun to see their role with increasing clarity. However grand it might sound, the fact is, they *are* confronting Empire in their own, very different ways. Differently in Iraq, in South Africa, in India, in Argentina, and differently, for that matter, on the streets of Europe and the United States. Mass resistance movements, individual activists, journalists, artists and film makers have come together to strip Empire of its sheen (Roy 2004, 3).

The United States must become a villager and give up being a giant. As Roy makes clear, this fact is more transparent for those outside the United States than those inside (Roy 2004; Hertsgaard 2002; Bellamy Foster and McChesney 2004; Chomsky 2003).

The third and fourth tasks actually dovetail. There is reason to believe that the productivist imperative of be all you can be is gendered—that is, it's a male-derived value. Since patriarchy and civilization began at the same time, we should perhaps view productivism and male domination in the same way. They have evolved in tandem and exist that way today. Of course, even though men and women have assimilated the imperative, at least in the developed world, one important front for activism is to end patriarchy. It's a vital necessity for its own sake, as there will be no sustainable future without gender justice, but it may also contribute in no small way to getting us beyond the imperative of being more. And ending patriarchy may be the best way to address population pressure. There is ample evidence from a variety of polls and surveys worldwide that most women, especially in the undeveloped nations, do *NOT* want to be pregnant and have more children. But because of male domination and women's economic dependence on men, they have children they would not otherwise have. Helping women achieve more economic independence from men, through micro lending to rural women for establishing their own businesses, for example, has had significant benefits for both ending patriarchal domination and population stabilization. Empowering women through economic independence may prove to be the best solution to reducing global population pressure.

A sustainable future requires that we grope our way to both a steady-state for population as well as output per person. By addressing both sides of the ecological footprint, we will be able to discover what is sustainable for humans in the community of life. These four challenges demand immediate attention by all of us as global citizens. None of the four are specifically tasks for either those in the have nations or those in the have-not nations. These are truly collective self-help issues for all global citizens.

One of the most therapeutic activities that will help us cope and be less stressed is simply to participate in whatever way we can in the process of social change. Whether or not we see a new world in our lifetime, to know that it is possible and to participate is enough—for now. It's not about "being more" as you act to lend a hand. By participating and trying to change a couple of minds you are demonstrating global responsibility. If such participation suggests to you that you are trying to be all you can be, that's fine. If it takes you trying to be more to help create a world in which being is enough, whoever said social change happens without contradictions?

References

AIS (American Institute of Stress). [cited 16 January 2005]. (http://www.stress.org).

Allen, David. 2001. *Getting Things Done: The Art of Stress-free Productivity*. New York: Penguin Putnam.

Aristotle. 1982. *Aristotle: Selected Works*. Translated by Hippocrates Apostle and Lloyd Gerson. Grinnell, IA: Paripatetic Press.

Atwood, J. Brian, and Michael Barnett. 2004. For a safer world, reduce poverty around globe. *Arizona Daily Sun*, 21 November: A3.

Ayn Rand Institute. 2005. [cited 11 February 2005]. (http://www.aynrand.org).

Ayres, Ed. 1999. *God's Last Offer*. New York: Four Walls Eight Windows.

Becker, Elizabeth. 2004. Number of Hungry Rising, U.N. Says. [cited 8 December 2004]. (http://www.nytimes.com/2004/12/08/international/08hunger).

Bell, Daniel. 1976. *The Coming of Post-Industrial Society*. Reissue Edition. New York: Basic Books.

Bellamy Foster, John, and Robert McChesney, eds. 2004. *Pox Americana: Exposing the American Empire*. New York: Monthly Review Press.

Bluestone, Barry, and Bennett Harrison. 1982. *The Deindustrialization of America*. New York: Basic Books.

———. 1988. *The Great U-Turn*. New York: Basic Books.

Bolles, Richard Nelson. 1994. *What Color Is Your Parachute?* Berkeley, CA: Ten Speed Press.

Bowles, Samuel, and David Gordon, and Thomas Weisskopf. 1984. *Beyond the Wasteland*. Garden City, NY: Anchor Press.

Boulding, Kenneth. 1975. Earth as a Spaceship. *Collected Papers of Kenneth Boulding*. Boulder, CO: University of Colorado Press.

Braverman, Harry. 1974. *Labor and Monopoly Capital*. New York: Monthly Review Press.

Bronowski, Jacob. 1973. *The Ascent of Man*. New York: Little, Brown.

Brown, Lester. 2001. *Eco-Economy*. New York: W.W. Norton.

———. 2003. *Plan B: Rescuing a Planet under Stress and a Civilization in Trouble*. New York: W.W. Norton.

Brumbaugh, Robert. 1964. *The Philosophers of Greece*. New York: Thomas Y. Crowell.

Cameron, Rondo. 1989. *A Concise Economic History of the World*. New York: Oxford University Press.

Chomsky, Noam. 2003. *Hegemony or Survival*. New York: Metropolitan Books.

Chouinard, Yvon. 2004. On Corporate Responsibility for Planet Earth. *Patagonia Pro Program: The Edge Book.* Ventura, CA: Patagonia, 37.

Collins, James. 2000. Built to Flip. *Fast Company,* March: 131-140.

Collins, James, and Jerry Porras. 1994. *Built to Last.* New York: HarperCollins.

CorpWatch (Corporate Watch). 2005. Top 200: The Rise of Corporate Global Power. [cited 8 March 2005]. (http://www.corpwatch.org/article.php?id=377).

Cranston, Maurice. 1967. Francis Bacon. *The Encyclopedia of Philosophy.* Vol. 1. Edited by Paul Edwards. New York: Macmillan, 235-240.

Davies, Brian. 1992. *The Thought of Thomas Aquinas.* Oxford: Clarendon Press.

Davis, Martha, Matthew McKay, and Elizabeth Eshelman. 2000. *The Relaxation and Stress Reduction Workbook.* 5th ed. Oakland, CA: New Harbinger.

De Graaf, John, David Wann, and Thomas Naylor. 2001. *Affluenza: The All-Consuming Epidemic.* San Francisco: Berrett-Koehler.

Drucker, Peter. 1992. *Managing the Non-Profit Organization.* Reprint Edition. New York: HarperCollins.

Earth Charter. 2005. [cited 8 March 2005]. (http://www.earthcharter.org).

Elgin, Duane. 1993. *Voluntary Simplicity.* New York: William Morrow.

Elkin, Allen. 1999. *Stress Management for Dummies.* Hoboken, NJ: For Dummies.

Ewen, Stuart. 1976. *Captains of Consciousness.* New York: McGraw-Hill.

Ewen, Stuart, and Elizabeth Ewen. 1982. *Channels of Desire.* New York: McGraw-Hill.

Feher, Ferenc, and Agnes Heller. 1988. *The Postmodern Political Condition.* New York: Columbia University Press.

Foucault, Michel. 1986. Of Other Spaces. *Diacritics.* Vol. 16, No. 1: 22-26.

Frankena, William. 1965. *Philosophy of Education.* Toronto: Macmillan.

Friedman, Milton. [1962] 1982. *Capitalism and Freedom.* Chicago: University of Chicago Press.

Gandhi, M. K. 1990. *The Essential Writings of Mahatma Gandhi.* Edited by Raghavan Iyer. New York: Oxford University Press.

Gardner, Gary, Erik Assadourian, and Radhika Sarin. 2004. The State of Consumption Today. *State of the World 2004.* Edited by Linda Starke. New York: W.W. Norton.

Global Issues. 2005. [cited 2 February 2005]. (http://www.globalissues.com).

Gowdy, John, ed. 1998. *Limited Wants, Unlimited Means: A Reader on Hunter-Gatherer Economics and the Environment.* Washington, DC: Island Press.

Greer, Thomas. 1972. *A Brief History of Western Man.* New York: Harcourt Brace Jovanovich.

Harrington, Michael. 1970. *Socialism.* New York: Saturday Review Press.

Harvey, David. 1989. *The Condition of Postmodernity: An Enquiry into the Origins of Cultural Change*. Cambridge, MA: Basil Blackwell.

Hawken, Paul, Amory Lovins, and Hunter Lovins. 1999. *Natural Capitalism*. New York: Little, Brown and Company.

Heilprin, John. 2004. Bush stands by rejection of limits on greenhouse gases. *Arizona Daily Sun*, 7 November: A1.

Hertsgaard, Mark. *1998. Earth Odyssey: Around the World in Search of Our Environmental Future*. New York: Broadway Books.

———. 2002. *The Eagle's Shadow: Why America Fascinates and Infuriates the World*. New York: Farrar, Straus and Giroux.

Hunt, E. K. 1990. *Property and Prophets*. New York: Harper and Row.

Jameson, Fredric. 1991. *Postmodernism: Or, The Cultural Logic of Late Capitalism*. Durham, NC: Duke University Press.

Kasser, Tim. 2002. *The High Price of Materialism*. Cambridge: MIT Press.

Kersten, Denise. 2002. Pursue your ideal career. *The Des Moines Register*, 16 December: D1.

Korten, David. 1999. *The Post-Corporate World*. West Hartford, CT: Kumarian Press.

Kunstler, James Howard. 1998. *Home From Nowhere*. Touchstone Edition. New York: Free Press.

Lash, Scott, and John Urry. 1987. *The End of Organized Capitalism*. Madison, WI: University of Wisconsin Press.

Lazarus, Judith. 2000. *Stress Relief and Relaxation Techniques*. New York: McGraw-Hill.

Lenzner, Robert, and Ashlea Ebeling. 1997. Peter Drucker's Picks. *Forbes Magazine*. Reprint Edition. 11 August 1997, 1-3.

Lim, Sunamita. 2002. Desert Rats, Mountain Men. *Sierra*. September/October, 67-68

Maslow, Abraham. 1968. *Toward a Psychology of Being*. New York: D. Van Nostrand.

Marx, Karl. 1978. *The Marx-Engels Reader*. Edited by Robert Tucker. New York: W.W. Norton.

McClaughry, John. 1989. Preface to the 1989 Edition. *Small Is Beautiful*. By E. F. Schumacher. New York: HarperCollins.

Mill, John Stuart. 1966. *John Stuart Mill: A Selection of His Works*. Edited by John M. Robson. New York: Odyssey Press.

Permaculture Activist. 2005. What is a Bioregion? [cited 14 February 2005]. (http://www.permacultureactivist.net).

Polanyi, Karl. [1944] 1957. *The Great Transformation: The Political and Economic Origins of Our Time*. Boston: Beacon Press.

Ponting, Clive. 1991. *A Green History of the World*. New York: St. Martin's Press.

Quinn, Daniel. 1992. *Ishmael*. New York: Bantam Books.

————. 1996. *The Story of B*. New York: Bantam Books.

————. 1997. *My Ishmael*. New York: Bantam Books.

————. 1999. *Beyond Civilization*. New York: Harmony Books.

Rifkin, Jeremy. 1991. *Biosphere Politics*. San Francisco: HarperCollins.

————. 2000. *The Age of Access*. New York: Tarcher/Putnam.

————. 2002. *The Hydrogen Economy*. New York: Tarcher/Putnam.

————. 2004. *The European Dream*. New York: Tarcher/Penguin.

Roy, Arundhati. 2004. People vs. Empire. [cited 7 December 2004]. (http://www.inthesetimes.com/site/main/print/people_vs_empire/).

Sahlins, Marshall. 1972. *Stone Age Economics*. New York: Aldine.

Scherer, Ron. 2005. Mergers return to style. *Arizona Daily Sun*, 6 February: D1.

Schnitzer, Martin. 2000. *Comparative Economic Systems*. Cincinnati: South-Western.

Schor, Juliet. 1992. *The Overworked American*. New York: Basic Books.

————. 1998. *The Overspent American*. New York: Basic Books.

————. 2004. *Born to Buy: The Commercialized Child and the New Consumer Culture*. New York: Scribner.

Schumacher, E. F. 1973. *Small Is Beautiful*. New York: Harper and Row.

Seneca. 1967. *Ad Lucilium Epistulae Morales*. Vol. 1. Translated by Richard Gummere. Cambridge: Harvard University Press.

Shah, Anup. 2005. Causes of Poverty. [cited 7 March 2005]. (http://www.globalissues.com).

Shiva, Vandana. 2005. Earth Democracy/Living Democracy. [cited 8 March 2005]. (http://www.vshiva.net).

Soja, Edward. 1989. *Postmodern Geographies: The Reassertion of Space in Critical Social Theory*. New York: Verso.

Sutel, Seth. 2005. P&G acquiring Gillette for $57B. *Arizona Daily Sun*, 29 January: A8.

Ulich, Robert. 1967. John Amos Comenius. *The Encyclopedia of Philosophy*. Vol. 2. Edited by Paul Edwards. New York: Macmillan, 146-147.

UNCTAD (United Nations Conference on Trade and Development). 2001. Conference on Least Developed Countries. [cited 2 February 2005]. (http://www.unctad.org/en/docs/aconf191d13).

Veblen, Thorstein. [1899] 1945. *The Theory of the Leisure Class*. New York: Viking Press.

Wallerstein, Immanuel. 1974. *The Modern World System.* Vol. 1. New York: Academic Press.

————. 1980. *The Modern World System.* Vol. 2. New York: Academic Press.

————. 2004. U.S. Weakness and the Struggle for Hegemony. *Pox Americana: Exposing the American Empire.* Edited by John Bellamy Foster and Robert McChesney. New York: Monthly Review Press, 41-50.

Walljasper, Jay. 2003. Ourselves: Are you more important than your appointment book? *Utne.* January: 61-63.

Whitehead, Alfred North. 1979. *Process and Reality.* New York: Free Press.

World Development Report 2003. Sustainable Development in a Dynamic World. The World Bank. New York: Oxford University Press.

Wolfe, Eric. 1997. *Europe and the People Without History.* Berkeley: University of California Press.

Wyse, Elizabeth, and Barry Winkleman, eds. [1988] 1997. *Past Worlds: Atlas of Archaeology.* London: HarperCollins.

YES! A Journal of Positive Futures. Bainbridge Island, WA: The Positive Futures Network.

Index

Seneca, 95-6
Shang dynasty, 94
Shiva, Vandana, 125, 130
Small Is Beautiful, 128
Smith, Adam, x, 39, 76, 117, 139
Social Democracy, 77
Social Security, xii, 20, 136
socialism, xi, 99-100, 126
South Africa, 57, 149
Soviet Union, 76, 119
St. Augustine, 96
St. Thomas Aquinas, 96
State of the World 2004, 108
steady-state economy, 142-3
Stone-Age Economics, 86
Story of B, The, 10
Stress Management for Dummies, 29
Stress Relief and Relaxation Techniques, 29
student development, 60
suffering, existential, dignified or undignified, 142-3
Summa Theologica, 96

taker civilization, 73-7, 125
taker thunderbolt, 74-5
taker(s), takerism, 39, 71-5, 77, 80-7, 94, 98, 103, 107, 112, 121, 125-6, 128, 145-7. *See also* driven takers, taker civilization.
Thich Nhat Hanh, 128
Tigris and Euphrates, 71
time scarcity, 7, 27
time-space compression, 67
Toward a Psychology of Being, 100
Toynbee, Arnold, 56

UN Declaration of Human Rights, 137
UN Human Development Report, 111
unions, 39, 77, 137, 139
United Methodist Church, 128
United Nations (UN), 111-2, 114, 130, 137-8
United Nations Commission on Trade and Development (UNCTAD), 111-2
Upper Paleolithic period, 80-1, 89-90
Utne magazine, 48, 125

Veblen, Thorstein, 61-2
Vietnam War, 113
voluntary simplicity movement, 21-2, 104, 125, 127, 142

Wallerstein, Immanuel, 76, 142
Walljasper, Jay, 48, 65, 125
water, overpumping, 109
Wealth of Nations, The, 76
welfare state, 19, 77
What Color is Your Parachute?, 52
Whitehead, Alfred North, 121-2
worker self-management, 126
World Bank, 111-2, 126, 130, 138
World Health Organization (WHO), 26, 112
World Social Forum, xi, 114, 142
World Watch Institute, 108

Yellow River, 3000 BC, 94
"You're on your own, pal," 12, 16, 18, 20, 37, 63, 77, 83, 98, 117

Zero Hunger Program, Brazil's, 130

About the Author

Doug Brown is professor of economics in the College of Business at Northern Arizona University in Flagstaff. He has been teaching courses in macro and microeconomics and comparative economic systems at NAU for twenty years after having completed his Ph.D. in economics at Colorado State University in 1985. Prior to this he taught at Denver Community College, the University of Montana, and Bellevue College in Omaha, Nebraska. His most recent book is *Insatiable Is Not Sustainable* (Westport, CT: Praeger, 2002). He has also edited a commemorative title on Thorstein Veblen, *Thorstein Veblen in the Twenty-First Century* (London: Edward Elgar, 1998). His articles on institutional economics, Marxism, social economics, and environmental philosophy have been published in journals including the *Review of Social Economics*, *Journal of Economic Issues*, and *Journal of Popular Culture*. As *Being* and *Insatiable* suggest, his most recent research concerns globalization of capitalism, social and environmental sustainability, and economic anthropology.